my **revision** notes

OCR AS

LAW

Andrew Shepherd

Jacqui Sparks

Ann Radford

Editor: Sue Teal

HODDER
EDUCATION

Orders: please contact Bookpoint Ltd, 130 Milton Park, Abingdon, Oxon OX14 4SB. Telephone: (44) 01235 827720. Fax: (44) 01235 400454. Lines are open from 9.00–5.00, Monday to Saturday, with a 24 hour message answering service. You can also order through our website **www.hoddereducation.co.uk**.

British Library Cataloguing in Publication Data
A catalogue record for this title is available from the British Library

ISBN: 9781444180534

First Published 2013
Impression number 10 9 8 7 6 5 4 3 2
Year   2016 2015 2014

Hachette UK's policy is to use papers that are natural, renewable and recyclable products and made from wood grown in sustainable forests. The logging and manufacturing processes are expected to conform to the environmental regulations of the country of origin.

Cover photo © 26ISO/iStockphoto
Typeset by CronosPro-Lt 12/14 points by Datapage (India) Pvt. Ltd.

Printed in India for Hodder Education, an Hachette UK company, 338 Euston Road, London NW1 3BH
London NW1 3BH.

Get the most from this book

Everyone has to decide his or her own revision strategy, but it is essential to review your work, learn it and test your understanding. These Revision Notes will help you to do that in a planned way, topic by topic. Use this book as the cornerstone of your revision and don't hesitate to write in it — personalise your notes and check your progress by ticking off each section as you revise.

☑ **Tick to track your progress**

Use the revision planner on pages 4–6 to plan your revision, topic by topic. Tick each box when you have:

● revised and understood a topic

● tested yourself

● practised the exam questions and gone online to check your answers and complete the quick quizzes

My revision planner

G151 English Legal System			
Civil courts and other methods of dispute resolution	Revised	Tested	Exam ready
9 Introduction	☐	☐	☐
9 The jurisdiction of the civil courts of first instance	☐	☐	☐
10 How a case is taken to court	☐	☐	☐
11 The track system	☐	☐	☐

You can also keep track of your revision by ticking off each topic heading in the book. You may find it helpful to add your own notes as you work through each topic.

Features to help you succeed

Exam tips and summaries

Throughout the book there are tips to help you boost your final grade.

Summaries provide advice on how to approach each topic in the exams.

Comments analyse student responses to exam questions, explaining why a student response will receive a certain grade.

Typical mistakes

Examples of typical mistakes candidates make and how you can avoid them.

Key terms

Clear, concise definitions of essential key terms are provided on the page where they appear.

Exam practice

Practice exam questions are provided for each topic. Use them to consolidate your revision and practise your exam skills.

Now test yourself

These short, knowledge-based questions provide the first step in testing your learning. Answers are at the back of the book.

Student activity

Use these questions to improve your knowledge and understanding.

Online

Go online to check your answers to the exam practice questions and try out the extra quick quizzes at **www.therevisionbutton.co.uk/ myrevisionnotes**

Check your understanding

Use the questions that have been set at the end of the topic to make sure that you understand each topic. Answers are at the back of the book.

How to answer

The examiner gives guidance on how to answer essay and scenario questions.

My revision planner

Exam practice answers and quick quizzes at **www.therevisionbutton.co.uk/myrevisionnotes**

Countdown to my exams

6–8 weeks to go

- Start by looking at the specification — make sure you know exactly what material you need to revise and the style of the examination. Use the revision planner on pages 4–6 to familiarise yourself with the topics.
- Organise your notes, making sure you have covered everything on the specification. The revision planner will help you to group your notes into topics.
- Work out a realistic revision plan that will allow you time for relaxation. Set aside days and times for all the subjects that you need to study, and stick to your timetable.
- Set yourself sensible targets. Break your revision down into focused sessions of around 40 minutes, divided by breaks. These Revision Notes organise the basic facts into short, memorable sections to make revising easier.

Revised ☐

4–6 weeks to go

- Read through the relevant sections of this book and refer to the exam tips, exam summaries, typical mistakes and key terms. Tick off the topics as you feel confident about them. Highlight those topics you find difficult and look at them again in detail.
- Test your understanding of each topic by working through the 'Now test yourself' and 'Check your understanding' questions in the book. Look up the answers at the back of the book.
- Make a note of any problem areas as you revise, and ask your teacher to go over these in class.
- Look at past papers. They are one of the best ways to revise and practise your exam skills. Write or prepare planned answers to the exam practice questions provided in this book. Check your answers online and try out the extra quick quizzes at **www.therevisionbutton.co.uk/myrevisionnotes**
- Try different revision methods. For example, you can make notes using mind maps, spider diagrams or flash cards.
- Track your progress using the revision planner and give yourself a reward when you have achieved your target.

Revised ☐

One week to go

- Try to fit in at least one more timed practice of an entire past paper and seek feedback from your teacher, comparing your work closely with the mark scheme.
- Check the revision planner to make sure you haven't missed out any topics. Brush up on any areas of difficulty by talking them over with a friend or getting help from your teacher.
- Attend any revision classes put on by your teacher. Remember, he or she is an expert at preparing people for examinations.

Revised ☐

The day before the examination

- Flick through these Revision Notes for useful reminders, for example the exam tips, exam summaries, typical mistakes and key terms.
- Check the time and place of your examination.
- Make sure you have everything you need — extra pens and pencils, tissues, a watch, bottled water, sweets.
- Allow some time to relax and have an early night to ensure you are fresh and alert for the examinations.

Revised ☐

My exams

AS Law G151

Date: ....

Time: ....

Location:.......................................

AS Law G152

Date: ....

Time: ....

Location:.......................................

G151 English Legal System

1 Civil courts and other methods of dispute resolution

This topic can be broken down into the following areas:
- The jurisdiction of the civil courts of first instance
- How a case is taken to court
- The track system
- The appellate courts
- Civil Court assessment including effects of the Woolf Reforms.

Two main skills are needed:
- The ability to describe, in detail, each of the above elements.
- The ability to analyse central issues and develop clear arguments.

Introduction

Following Lord Woolf's recommendations for reform of the civil justice system in his report *Access to Justice* (1996) and the 1999 Civil Procedure rules, before taking a matter to court, parties are encouraged to use alternative dispute resolution (ADR). Even if the claim has started, a judge can 'stay' proceedings in order that a form of ADR is attempted. In certain cases, Pre-Action Protocols encourage parties to take certain steps before the proceedings start.

The jurisdiction of the civil courts of first instance

There are two civil courts of first instance:
- the County Court
- the High Court.

The County Court

There are approximately 220 County Courts in England and Wales and these courts have the jurisdiction to hear, for example:
- contract, tort, recovery of land to any value
- partnerships, trusts, and inheritance up to £30,000
- divorce and bankruptcy
- personal injury less than £50,000
- small claims, fast-track and some multi-track cases.

The High Court

The High Court is based in London; however there are several district registries of the High Court in major towns and cities. The High Court is divided into three divisions and each division has jurisdiction to hear certain matters. The three divisions are:

- Queen's Bench Division
- Family Division
- Chancery Division.

Queen's Bench Division (QBD)

The QBD has jurisdiction to hear contract and tort cases over £50,000 and some complex multi-track cases. The QBD also contains the Commercial Court, the Admiralty Court and the Technology and Construction Court. The QBD has a supervisory role and hears judicial review.

Family Division (FD)

This court has jurisdiction to hear wardship cases, cases under the Children Act 1989 and other family matters.

Chancery Division (CD)

This court deals with technical issues and has jurisdiction to hear matters of insolvency, mortgages, trusts, property disputes, copyright and patents, intellectual property and probate disputes.

> **Exam tip**
>
> To answer a question on the Civil Courts you need to be able to do more than simply name the courts. You must be able to show good knowledge and understanding of the main types of cases that can be heard in the County Court and the High Court.

Check your understanding

1 Identify three cases the County Court has jurisdiction to hear.
2 Identify two cases the Chancery Division has jurisdiction to hear.
3 Identify two cases the Family Court has jurisdiction to hear.
4 Identify two courts contained in the Queen's Bench Division.

Answers on p.130

How a case is taken to court

Revised

Starting a claim

Most people will not go to court if they can avoid it and some form of negotiation will usually take place. However, if this fails the claimant must do the following:

- Complete and submit to the court a N1 Claim Form naming the defendant and stating the particulars of the claim, including the amount of damages being sought.
- The court will send the N1 to the defendant and they are given the opportunity to admit the claim and pay the amount claimed or defend the claim.
- If the defendant chooses to defend the claim, the court will send an allocation questionnaire to both the parties.
- When the claimant returns this questionnaire a fee must be paid. The fee depends on the amount being claimed.
- Some claims can be made online using the Ministry of Justice's 'Money Claim Online' website. However you can only use this if your claim is for a fixed amount of less than £100,000.

The track system

The information on the questionnaire dictates which of the three tracks the case will be allocated to. It can be allocated to the:

- small-claims track
- fast track
- multi-track.

Small-claims track

- Hears contract and tort cases worth up to £5,000 and personal injury cases up to £1,000.
- Strict time limit for cross-examination of witnesses.
- Heard by a District Judge in the County Court.
- Informal and use of lawyers discouraged.

Fast track

- Hears claims from £5,000 to £25,000.
- Strict timetable set – case should be heard within 30 weeks.
- Trial to last one day and limited number of witnesses.
- Heard by a District Judge in the County Court.

Multi-track

- Hears claims over £25,000 or cases involving complex points.
- Heard by a Circuit Judge in the County Court but can be sent to the High Court.
- Judge will 'case manage', setting a strict timetable for matters such as disclosure of documents.
- Parties may be encouraged to try one of the alternative methods of dispute resolution.

> **Exam tip**
>
> Many candidates miss out on valuable marks in questions on civil court procedure because they usually know the track system but not the jurisdiction of the courts as stated above. The results of this omission may be to only get 50% of the available marks!

Check your understanding

5 Describe briefly what procedure the claimant must follow in order to have their claim allocated to a court.

6 Identify the judge and court hearing a small claims case.

7 What is the maximum amount of money that can be claimed for a contract case in the small claims court?

8 What is the maximum period (in weeks) between directions and trial date for a fast-track case?

9 Identify the judge and court hearing a fast-track case.

10 When will a case under £25,000 be heard in the High Court?

11 Identify the judge and court hearing a multi-track case.

Answers on p.130

The Appellate Courts

There are three appellate courts in the English legal system; they are:

- The Divisional Courts of the High Court
- The Court of Appeal (Civil Division)
- The Supreme Court.

The Divisional Courts of the High Court

As stated above, the High Court has three Divisions and all three Divisions hear appeals from other courts as well as first instance cases.

Queen's Bench Division (QBD)

The QBD has two main appellate functions:

- To preside over applications for judicial review which are proceedings in which a judge reviews the lawfulness of a decision or action made by a public body.
- To hear appeals by way of case stated from criminal matters decided in the Magistrates' Court.

Court of Appeal (Civil Division)

The Court of Appeal (Civil Division) is headed by the Master of the Rolls and hears appeals from:

- divisions of the High Court
- some County Courts' multi-track cases
- certain tribunals.

In order to bring an appeal to this court, 'permission' (leave) is needed. This can be granted by the court below or by the Court of Appeal itself.

Supreme Court

The Supreme Court is the final court of appeal in the English legal system and hears cases of public importance. It hears cases from:

- Courts of Appeal
- Divisional Courts
- High Court under the 'leap frog' provisions.

In order to bring an appeal to this court, 'permission' (leave) is needed and this can be granted by the Supreme Court itself or the lower courts.

Civil Court assessment including effects of the Woolf Reforms (AO2)

Revised

Civil Court assessment

The introduction of the Woolf Reforms in April 1999 overhauled the Civil Procedure Rules and brought about many changes to the civil courts. Some of the effects of the Woolf Reforms are as follows, and you will note that not all are positive effects:

- There is now more co-operation between parties and case management has been a success and there is a high rate of settlement before the hearing, reaching almost 80% in some areas.
- Rules on disclosure and time are very strictly enforced and in fast-track cases there are limitations on expert witnesses. This ensures that cases are dealt with quickly. One may question whether such strictness allows for justice?
- Early settlement is actively encouraged by the use of pre-action protocols and the encouragement of the use of alternative dispute resolution. However, there has not been the large increase in the use of ADR as expected.

Exam practice answers and quick quizzes at **www.therevisionbutton.co.uk/myrevisionnotes**

- Allocation questionnaires and case management conferences ensure that parties know how the case is to be managed and the number of witnesses allowed, however these are complex and time-consuming.

- Some say that delays between issuing a claim and the hearing have reduced; however, there are mixed views about this and some say delay is still a problem in comparison with alternative dispute resolution methods. Fast-track cases can still take 48 weeks to get to trial which can hardly be called 'fast', but is faster than before the reforms, and even small claims can take 29 weeks to be heard. Multi-track cases can still sometimes take years to get to court.

- Costs have increased overall due to the front-loading of costs for the fast-track and the multi-track. There is a lack of legal funding for small claims and limitations for other cases (and funding is being taken away from more and more cases).

- Court remains very formal and this can be intimidating to some individuals.

- The courts are still under-resourced, with IT systems regarded as primitive in comparison with private practice.

Small claims track assessment

There are many advantages and disadvantages of bringing a case to the small claims court, for example:

Advantages	Disadvantages
The cost of taking a claim is low if the claim is under £1,000.	Legal funding is not available for small claims.
The District Judge is supposed to help the parties to explain their case and to make the process inquisitorial rather than adversarial.	Research shows that the District Judge is not always as helpful as expected when dealing with unrepresented claimants.
If you lose you do not have to pay the other person's legal costs.	The decision is difficult to enforce and if you win you only have a 60% chance of being paid what the court has awarded.
A lawyer is not required and the claimant can represent themselves.	Businesses tend to use lawyers and this puts an unrepresented individual at a distinct disadvantage.

Typical mistakes

- Only answering half the question – usually knowing the track system but not the jurisdiction of the courts – this means you'll only get half the marks.
- Including the appeal courts when the question specifically asks for you to describe the jurisdiction of the civil courts of first instance.
- Answering a question on ADR, although it is not on the paper, because that was revised for!

How to avoid those mistakes

- Ensure you read the question properly – look out for the words 'civil' or 'criminal'.
- Ensure you know the jurisdiction of each of the courts – what is heard in the County Court and Divisions of the High Court.
- Revise the topics thoroughly.

Exam tip

Questions tend to be either on civil appeals or the jurisdiction of the courts and the track system. These are ideal questions to tackle if you have good recall skills. Make sure you read the question carefully so that you give the correct information.

Student activity

Create a booklet to help those who wish to make a civil claim

Produce an information booklet that will give guidance to a person wishing to make a civil claim. The following points should be considered:

1 What to do/try before going to court.

2 What is the jurisdiction of the civil courts – which court should be used for different types of case?

3 How to issue a claim.

4 What sort of responses might there be from the other side?

5 How does the track system work?

6 How will a case be allocated to a track and by whom?

7 How much is it likely to cost?

8 How long is it likely to take and what happens between issuing the claim and the trial date?

9 How long will the trial itself take?

10 What is the appeals process if you are not successful?

Exam practice

A question on the civil courts

a) Describe the jurisdiction of both the High Court and the County Court in civil cases, including the track system. **[18 marks]**

b) Discuss the advantages and disadvantages of the small claims track. **[12 marks]**
   OCR G151 January 2010

Answers and quick quizzes online

Online

Alternative dispute resolution (ADR)

Revised

The knowledge required in this subject relates to three key areas:

- Mediation
- Conciliation
- Arbitration.

Three main skills are needed:

- The ability to describe each of the three elements.
- The ability to give at least one example of each.
- The ability to analyse central issues and develop clear arguments.

What is ADR?

Alternative dispute resolution (ADR) is a mechanism used in order to resolve a dispute without a court hearing.

Why is there a need for ADR?

Court hearings are not always the most appropriate or best method of dealing with a civil dispute. Court cases are expensive, time consuming and can be very traumatic due to the adversarial nature of the hearing. Having

> **Exam tip**
>
> It is possible to get full marks in an alternative dispute resolution question without describing negotiation as that is not specifically mentioned in the specification. However, negotiation is often used as a way of introducing the topic.

a winner and a loser often leads to the breakdown of the relationship between the parties, be it business or family. The different forms of ADR offer the chance of avoiding some of the problems associated with court hearings.

Assessment of ADR

Revised

Advantages of ADR

- **Costs** – ADR is usually cheaper to solve disputes as there are no court costs incurred.
- **Speed** – ADR will allow matters to be resolved more quickly than going through a court hearing.
- **Control** – the parties have more control over ADR rather than handing control to the courts.
- **Flexibility** – the time and place can be arranged to suit both parties resulting in a more informal and relaxed hearing. The strict letter of the law does not need to be followed.
- **Expertise** – the parties can choose their own mediator/conciliator/arbitrator – e.g. a technical expert.
- **Privacy** – the matter will be dealt with in private and therefore no publicity.
- ADR is **less adversarial** than court hearings and encourages co-operation. This allows relationships, e.g. business relationships, to continue (avoiding bad feelings). They are often destroyed by the adversarial nature of a court hearing.

Disadvantages of ADR

- **Unequal bargaining power** – in some matters one party is able to dominate the other, for example, in employment cases or divorce. In such circumstances, a tribunal or court may be the better option.
- **Lack of legal expertise** – during the process a legal issue may arise and the mediator/conciliator/arbitrator may lack the legal expertise to deal with it.
- **Court action may still be required** – following the mediation/conciliation process, the matter may still remain unresolved and therefore will need to go to court. This takes time and money.
- **Lack of enforceability** – in terms of mediation and conciliation, the agreement is usually unenforceable. If one party fails to fulfil the terms of the agreement, the matter may still have to go before the court.

> **Exam tip**
>
> It is important to read questions carefully. In Section A (b) 'discuss'-style questions, you may be asked to simply discuss the advantages and/or disadvantages of ADR in general or you may be asked to discuss a specific type of ADR in comparison to either another form of ADR or the Courts.

Mediation

Revised

Mediation is a voluntary process where an impartial/neutral third party (mediator) will assist the parties in coming to a compromise solution. The parties control the process, with the mediator playing a passive role and acting as a facilitator, allowing the parties to reach their own agreement. The mediator will be in charge of the process but will not influence the outcome. This agreement/outcome is not binding unless formally recorded in a signed agreement. The process can be terminated by either party at any stage.

A more formal method of mediation is the Formalised Settlement Conference. This involves a mini-trial, with a panel of three mediators. The panel is made up of one decision-making executive from each party and a neutral mediator to assist if necessary.

Examples of mediation services

There is a growing number of local and national mediation services, for example:

- The Centre for Effective Dispute Resolution (CEDR). CEDR offers dispute resolution solutions to a wide range people from large businesses to small private clients.

- Family Mediators Association – offers comprehensive family and hybrid mediation.

Exam tip

Although the mediation process is voluntary, from 6 April 2011 all divorcing and separating couples wishing to obtain legal funding have been referred to mediation to try and settle any disputes before being allowed to go to court.

Conciliation

Revised

Conciliation is very similar to mediation in that it is voluntary and both parties must agree to submit their matter to the conciliation process. As in mediation, the conciliator has no power to impose their own solution but they will play a far more active role than a mediator by suggesting grounds for compromise and possible ways of resolving the issue. The final agreement is not legally binding on either party unless made so by a signed agreement.

Example of a conciliation service

The Advisory, Conciliation and Arbitration Service (ACAS) deals with employment matters.

Assessment of mediation and conciliation

Revised

Advantages

- Voluntary process, encourages co-operation and avoids the adversarial system.
- Both can be cheap and quick.
- Less formal than court proceedings and does not have to follow the strict letter of the law.
- Maintains working relationships and can include decisions about future dealings.
- Both parties maintain a sense of control and can choose the method of mediation.
- Agreements are more likely to last as they are a compromise and in a sense 'everyone wins'.
- Highly successful.
- Private and no media exposure.
- Mediation and arbitration organisations have experts to assist.

Disadvantages

- No guarantee that the dispute will be resolved.
- Will not work unless both parties are willing to co-operate and reach a compromise.

Exam practice answers and quick quizzes at **www.therevisionbutton.co.uk/myrevisionnotes**

- Settlements are often considerably lower than those awarded by the courts.
- Agreements cannot be enforced, so there is no pressure to stick to it.
- Could go on for a long time without a settlement.
- Unless the mediator has the necessary qualities, mediation can turn in to a bullying exercise and weaker parties may not stand up for their own rights.

Arbitration

Revised

Arbitration is the most formal method of ADR whereby both parties will voluntarily agree to:

- allow their dispute be left to the judgment of an independent/neutral arbitrator or a panel of arbitrators
- the time and place of the hearing
- the procedure for the hearings – this can range from a 'paper' arbitration to a formal court-like hearing
- be legally bound by the arbitrator's decision – the 'Award'.

If required, the decision can be enforced by the courts. The Award is final; however, it can be challenged in the courts for serious irregularity in the proceedings or on a point of law.

Agreements to arbitrate are governed by the Arbitration Act 1996 and are usually in writing. Agreement to go to arbitration can be made before a dispute arises as per a *Scott v Avery* clause in a contract. These clauses are often seen in building or business contracts. The agreement will either name an arbitrator or provide a method for choosing one. A court may also appoint an arbitrator.

Examples of arbitration services

- The Advisory, Conciliation and Arbitration Service (ACAS) – deals with employment matters.
- The Association of British Travel Agents (ABTA) Arbitration scheme deals with alleged breaches of contract and/or negligence between consumers and Members of ABTA in respect of holidays.

Assessment of arbitration

Revised

Advantages

- The parties can choose their arbitrator and appoint a technical expert if appropriate.
- Use of an expert to decide avoids having to use expert witnesses.
- Flexibility – the time and place of the hearing can be decided by the parties to suit their needs and is held in private.
- Confidentiality.
- Likely to be dealt with quicker and cheaper than the courts.
- Award is final and can be enforced by the courts.
- Avoidance of bad feeling between the parties.

Disadvantages

- Unexpected legal points may crop up which the arbitrator may not be able to fully take into account.
- When dealing with technical points, arbitration may become highly complex.
- Commercial arbitration can take as long as the courts to complete.
- Professional arbitrators may be very expensive.
- The lack of availability of legal funding may disadvantage an individual.
- Rights of appeal are more limited than the courts.

Now test yourself

Tested

See if you can answer the following question using the P, D, W formula explained above.

1 Discuss the advantages and disadvantages of using mediation and conciliation rather than using the courts? (12 marks)

Point	Developed	Well developed
An advantage of both mediation and conciliation is that it is a voluntary method of dealing with an issue. You are not forced to partake.		
An advantage of using both mediation and conciliation is that it is likely to be a much quicker process than going through the courts.		
A disadvantage of mediation and conciliation is that a party may not get as much as they deserve as settlements are often lower than those awarded by the court.		
A disadvantage of mediation and conciliation is that the agreement is not legally binding.		

Answers on p.130

Tested

2   Match the statement with the correct answer.

Statement	Answer
An organisation devoted to preventing and resolving employment disputes	Due to increased delays and costs
The name given to the methods of dealing with civil matters without going to court	Commercial issues
This form of ADR is governed by statute	Privacy
The name of the Act of Parliament governing arbitration	Employment disputes
The name of the decision made by the arbitrator(s)	Relationship issues
Arbitration is particularly helpful when dealing with these sorts of matters	Mediation
The form of ADR where the third party plays an active role in helping the parties come to a compromise	The Centre for Effective Dispute Resolution (CEDR)
A reason arbitration is becoming unpopular	Alternative Dispute Resolution (ADR)
Conciliation is particularly helpful when dealing with these sorts of matters	Arbitration Act
An example of a formal method of approaching mediation	When divorcing and separating couples are referred before being allowed to go to court
One of the main disadvantages of mediation and conciliation	Award
The form of ADR where the third party remains passive	Advisory, Conciliation and Arbitration Service (ACAS)
One of the main advantages of all three types of ADR	Arbitration
Mediation is particularly helpful when dealing with these sorts of matters	Lack of binding agreement
An example of a commercial mediation service	Conciliation
When might mediation not be voluntary?	Formalised Settlement Conference

Answers on pp.130–131

Answers on pp.130–131

Exam practice

a) Describe the different methods of Alternative Dispute Resolution available to deal with civil cases.   [18 marks]

b) Discuss the advantages and disadvantages of using arbitration rather than using the courts.   [12 marks]

OCR G151 June 2010

Answers and quick quizzes online

Online

2 Criminal process

Police powers Revised ☐

The knowledge required in this chapter relates to the following four areas:

- Stop and search on the street
- Arrest
- Detention at the police station
- Searches and samples at the police station.

Three main skills are needed:

- An ability to describe in detail the law relating to each area for part (a) questions in both sections of the paper.
- Development of analytical and critical points for Section A part (b), discussion questions.
- Application of relevant law for Section B part (b), scenario questions.

What do you need to know about stop and search on the street? Revised ☐

The main piece of legislation that deals with stop and search is the Police and Criminal Evidence Act 1984 (PACE) as amended by the Codes of Practice and other relevant legislation.

Section 1 of PACE sets out that the police have the power to stop and search a person in a public place if they have reasonable suspicion that prohibited articles, stolen goods or articles made, adapted or intended for use in burglary or criminal damage are in their possession (prohibited fireworks were added in the Serious Organised Crime and Police Act 2005).

Many other statutes give power to the police to stop and search:

- The Misuse of Drugs Act 1971, which gives the power to search for prohibited drugs.
- The Terrorism Act 2000, where the police can ask for headgear and shoes to be removed, in addition to the outer coat, jacket and gloves permitted under PACE.
- Section 60 of the Criminal Justice and Public Order Act 1994 gives the police the power to stop and search anyone in an area designated by a senior officer for up to 24 hours in anticipation of violence. In this situation there does not have to be any reasonable suspicion that anything will be found, just being in that area at that time is enough for a stop and search to take place.

What is reasonable suspicion?

Code of Practice A sets out guidance for police on reasonable suspicion and states it cannot be based on personal appearance or criminal record

> **Exam tip**
>
> It is important to read the question carefully. If it asks for a description of the powers of the police under a specific piece of legislation such as PACE 1984, the answer should be limited to that legislation as there will be no credit for information about other legislation. If the legislation is not specified, legislation other than PACE should also be mentioned.

Exam practice answers and quick quizzes at **www.therevisionbutton.co.uk/myrevisionnotes**

alone. These can be taken into account, providing there are other reasons to suspect.

What are the rules that must be followed by the police when stopping and searching?

- The police officer must give his/her name, station and the reason for the search.
- Only certain clothing may be removed in public.
- There is no such thing as a 'voluntary search' – there must be a statutory power for any search.
- A written report required for every stop and search.

What sort of issues might be discussed in Section A part (b) questions?

The correct balance between individual rights and the need to combat crime is often used as a question. The following points may be useful.

- It is important to be able to ask people to remove items that may conceal their identity or help them avoid detection, as illustrated where a failed London bomber initially avoided detection dressed in a burka.
- Searching for prohibited items does prevent some crime – the Tottenham leaflet experiment led to a 50% reduction in stop and search but increases in both burglary and street robbery in the area, illustrating this point.
- The fact that the police officer has to identify him- or herself and give a reason for the search protects the individual from random searches, illustrated by *Osman* (1999).
- Code of Practice A setting out what is not reasonable suspicion should protect individuals from harassment because of their appearance or previous record, however reasonable suspicion is still very open ended and easy to justify.
- The fact that all searches must have statutory authority and a report must be written protects individuals as each search must be justified.
- Stop and search has increased tenfold since 1986 and only 10–13% of people stopped are then arrested.
- Many people do not know their rights which may make the rights ineffective.
- Section 60 of the Criminal Justice and Public Order Act tends to be misused to deal with street robbery or other crimes rather than its original purpose of dealing with riots.

Exam tip

Remember that a search always has to be in order to find something, so that you do not get confused with reasons for arresting a person on the street.

What do you need to know about arrest on the street?

Revised

The powers of the police are set out under Section 24 of the Police and Criminal Evidence Act 1984, as amended by the Serious Organised Crime and Police Act (SOCPA) 2005 and the Criminal Justice Act 2003, and the Codes of Practice (Code G).

Section 24 PACE, as amended by SOCPA 2005, sets out the power to arrest without a warrant. Code G gives guidelines for arrest.

The police have the power to arrest a person if:

- a person has committed an offence (past); or
- is in the act of committing an offence (present); or
- is about to commit an offence (future); or
- there are reasonable grounds for suspecting one of these occurrences (even if no offence is actually committed).

The police may use reasonable force to carry out the arrest.

The police have the power to search the arrested person for anything that may help them escape.

Other powers of arrest

- Arrest for breach of the peace (common law power) preserved by Section 26 PACE.
- Arrest for breaching bail conditions.
- Arrest with a warrant – Section 8 Magistrates Court Act 1980.
- Section 41 Terrorism Act 2000.
- There are many other powers of arrest, e.g. aggravated trespass under the Criminal Justice and Public Order Act 1994.

> **Exam tip**
>
> There are very many powers of arrest under different legislation. You should try to mention two or three unless a question is limited to PACE 1984.

Limitations   Revised ☐

The necessity test sets limits on when an officer has the power to arrest. The officer can only arrest if s/he has reasonable grounds for believing that it is necessary to make the arrest for one of the following reasons:

- To enable the name and address of suspect to be ascertained.
- To prevent the person causing physical injury to himself or any other person.
- Suffering physical injury.
- If someone is causing loss or damage to property.
- If someone is committing an offence against public decency.
- If someone is causing an unlawful obstruction of the highway.
- To protect a child or vulnerable person.
- To allow the prompt and effective investigation of the offence or the conduct of the person.
- To prevent any prosecution for the offence from being hindered by the disappearance of the person in question.
- The police must tell a person at the time of arrest, or as soon as practicable afterwards, why they are under arrest, the reason for arrest (no set words but it must be understandable, see *Taylor v Chief Constable of Thames Valley Police*), why the arrest is necessary and give a caution.
- They also have to identify themselves if not in uniform to make the arrest lawful.

Exam practice answers and quick quizzes at **www.therevisionbutton.co.uk/myrevisionnotes**

Now test yourself

1 What does PACE stand for?
2 What power does Section 1 of PACE give to the police?
3 What is illustrated by the case of *Osman* (1999)?
4 How does Code of Practice A describe reasonable suspicion?
5 What clothing can a police officer ask a person to remove in public?
6 What power does S60 CJPOA 1994 give to the police?
7 When can the police arrest without a warrant?
8 Which Act amended S24 of PACE?
9 What is the necessity test for arrest and when would arrest be regarded as necessary?
10 The person making the arrest must state what to the person being arrested?

Answers on p.131

Police powers to detain a suspect at the police station

- Where a person arrested on suspicion of a summary (less serious) offence, then the police can only detain them for a maximum of 24 hours.

- Where a person has been arrested on suspicion of an indictable (a more serious offence), then the police can detain for a further 12 hours (total of 36) with permission of a senior officer (superintendent or above).

- To detain a person beyond 36 hours for an indictable offence, the police must apply to the Magistrate's Court. The magistrate can order detention up to a maximum total of 96 hours.

- In cases where the suspect has been arrested for terrorism offences, the detention may be extended to 14 days by a magistrate.

Individual rights during detention

- The right to have a custody officer monitor detention and keep a custody record to ensure the Codes of Practice are adhered to.

- The right to have someone informed of the detention. (This can be delayed for up to 36 hours in exceptional circumstances for serious crimes.)

- If under the age of 17 or suffering any mental illness or retardation, the right to have a person responsible for their welfare informed of the arrest.

- The right to consult the Codes of Practice.

- The right to legal advice (which is free), although this is usually limited to telephone advice, and being allowed to consult privately with a solicitor.

- The right to an interpreter or medical treatment if necessary.

- The right to be released after 24 hours if the offence is less serious, unless charged,

- If the alleged offence is indictable, the right to be held only for 36 hours with permission of a police officer of the rank of superintendent or above.

- If the alleged offence is indictable, then the right to be held for a maximum of 96 hours but only if authorised by a magistrate.

- In suspected terrorism cases, the right to only be held for a maximum of 14 days.
- The right to have access to medical treatment if required.
- The right to be detained in an adequately heated, cleaned, lit and ventilated cell.
- The right to at least two light meals and one main meal in any 24 hours, plus drinks.
- In any period of 24 hours, a detainee must be given a continuous period of at least eight hours' rest.

Interviews   Revised ☐

- All interviews must be taped and a caution given.
- There is a right to have legal advice but this may be limited to advice via the phone.
- The presence of an appropriate adult is required in certain circumstances.
- The interview room must be heated to a reasonable temperature and breaks and refreshments must be provided.

For Section A part b) questions, you need to be able to comment on these points and:

- point out that legal advice is now often confined to the telephone, which may disadvantage many suspects
- that the aim of an interview has traditionally been in order to get a confession rather than necessarily to find out the truth.

Police powers to search a suspect at the police station   Revised ☐

- Police have the power to strip-search a suspect, but only if necessary to remove an article which a person in detention is not be allowed to keep and there is reasonable suspicion that the person might have such an article concealed on their person.
- A high-ranking police officer can authorise an intimate search if there is reason to believe that the suspect has with them an item which they could use to cause physical injury to themselves or others, or that they are in possession of a Class A drug.

Individual rights during searches   Revised ☐

- The right not to be automatically searched – searches can only be done in certain circumstances.
- The right only to be strip-searched if it is deemed necessary in order to remove an article which a person should not have.
- The right to have the strip-search carried out in a private place with a same-sex officer and only half the clothing removed at any one time.
- The right for an intimate search to only be carried out if authorised by a high-ranking officer in order to search for Class A drugs or weapons and to be carried out by a doctor or nurse.

Now test yourself

11 Fill in the following grid detailing powers of the police and rights of the individual at the police station.

Powers of the police	Limitations on powers	Individual rights
To detain individuals	Only for certain time limits...	Custody officer...
Can delay right to legal advice	Only if...	Right to legal advice...
Can delay right to inform	Only if...	Right to have someone informed of detention...
Can interview suspect	Must be taped and...	Appropriate adult for young offenders or if mental problems Interpreter if necessary Right to a solicitor
Can search suspect using one of three types of search: Check-in search Strip search Intimate search	Only if going to find something prohibited...	Must be done in particular way to protect privacy of suspect...
Can take samples	Non-intimate...	By... With permission from...
	Intimate...	By... With permission from...

Answers on p.131

Typical mistake

(In Section A part b) questions.)

- A failure to actually discuss anything and just to give information. There are no marks for pure information.
- It is also common to see answers where the candidate has made some attempt to discuss in a limited way by saying something is good or bad but without giving a reason.
- There is sometimes confusion about what the powers of the police are and what the rights of the individual are.
- Lack of evidence to back up any arguments.
- Lack of any conclusion to the answer.

Exam tip

How to answer discussion questions

- ✓ Comment on each point as you answer the question. Give reasons for your opinions.
- ✓ Use statistics and other evidence to back up your arguments.
- ✓ Cover all areas required by the question.
- ✓ Come to a conclusion at the end of your answer.
- ✓ For each of the five topics within police powers, you could be asked to discuss whether the powers of the police or the rights of the individual are: adequately protected/enough to do their job effectively/ balanced. You could also be asked to comment on any need for reform or whether recent reforms have been an improvement.
- ✓ Answer the question in a logical sequence.
- ✓ As you only have 10 minutes, you are likely to be asked about only one topic. State the law unless it was covered in part a), then comment on it point by point.
- ✓ Try to produce a balanced argument with at least four distinct points developed as far as you can.
- ✓ Ensure you are able to quote some statistics and have thought out arguments for all possible questions.

How to answer scenario questions

- Refer to the subject of the scenario throughout your answer.
- If the scenario does not mention something that would be necessary to make the police action lawful, comment on it, e.g. no mention of a police officer identifying themself in a stop and search,
- Use cases and examples, e.g. *Osman*, for the above situation.
- There should be at least five issues within the scenario for you to identify and apply the law to.
- Come to a conclusion based on the question for each issue.
- Be careful with samples as there is often one that is intimate and one that is non-intimate so they are separate and should not be dealt with together.

Typical mistake

Be very careful that you do revise the topic properly as many candidates like the topic and think they know it, but really do not remember the fine detail. Be extra careful to separate out powers of the police and their limitations from the rights of the individual, as that is by far the most common mistake.

3 Criminal courts

The knowledge required in this chapter relates to the following four areas:

- The categories of offence
- How the court of trial is chosen
- Bail
- Trial at first instance in the Magistrates' Court
- Trial at first instance in the Crown Court
- Appeals and challenges.

Three main skills are needed:

- An ability to describe in detail the law relating to each area for part (a) questions in both sections of the paper.
- Development of analytical and critical points for Section A part (b), discussion questions.
- Application of relevant law for Section B part (b), scenario questions.

Pre-trial matters
Revised

Categories of offence and choice of court

The three categories of offences are:

- **Summary offences** – less serious offences always tried in the Magistrates' Court, e.g. driving offences and common assault.
- **Triable-either-way (TEW) offences** – middle-range offences which can vary in the degree of harm caused. Can be tried either in the Magistrates' Court or in the Crown Court, e.g. theft and assault occasioning actual bodily harm.
- **Indictable offences** – more serious crimes which must be tried in the Crown Court, e.g. murder, manslaughter and rape.

> **Exam tip**
>
> Each category would need to be named with the relevant court or courts and an example should be given for each.

> **Typical mistake**
>
> There is usually good knowledge of examples of the categories of offences, although many times the examples are not all correct. (It is much better to have one correct example than two or three examples with one or more not being correct.) Theft is triable either way, no matter how small the theft.

What is the process for deciding which court a triable-either-way offence will be heard in?
Revised

1 Plea before venue – the defendant is asked whether (s)he pleads guilty or not guilty to the offence. If guilty, the case is automatically heard by the Magistrates' Court but the option is retained of sending the defendant to the Crown Court if necessary for sentencing.

2 If the defendant pleads not guilty, a mode of trial procedure must take place to decide on the most appropriate court to try the case.

3   The magistrates first consider whether they think the case is suitable for trial in the Magistrates' Court. If they feel it is not, they will transfer it to the Crown Court for trial. The defendant will have no choice.

4   If the magistrates feel prepared to accept jurisdiction of the case, the defendant is given the choice of which court (s)he wishes to be tried in.

Why would a defendant choose trial in the Magistrates' Court?

Revised

- There are restrictions on the possible penalties – a maximum fine of £5,000, and a maximum custodial sentence of six months, or twelve months for two or more TEW offences.
- It is much faster than the Crown Court, with most cases dealt with in less than one day.
- There is less publicity as these are seen as less serious crimes so journalists tend to spend their time at Crown Court.
- The court procedure is less daunting than Crown Court – less formal as there are no wigs and gowns used and no jury.

Why would a defendant choose trial in the Crown Court?

Revised

- There is a higher conviction rate in the Magistrates' Court. The acquittal rate in the Crown Court is over 50% but only 20% in the Magistrates' Court.
- Legal funding is less likely in the Magistrates' Court so the defendant may need to represent themselves which could be rather daunting.
- If the defendant is remanded in custody, time served will count against sentence and the conditions are better on remand.
- The benefits of using the Magistrates' Court for TEW matters may be lost when at the end, the magistrates decide they lack sentencing powers and send the matter to the Crown Court for sentencing.

Should the defendant be able to choose?

- There has been much debate about whether a defendant should have the choice and the choice has been limited by successive governments.
- It is much more expensive to hold jury trials.
- The government has limited trial by jury by reclassifying offences that were triable either way as summary, e.g. taking a vehicle without consent.
- The House of Lords has so far stopped government's attempts to abolish the defendant's right to choose as it felt that the right to jury trial is too important as a safeguard of liberty.
- Compromise has been made with cases that are felt too difficult for juries to understand, e.g. fraud, or if a jury has already been tampered with. These no longer have a jury although they are tried in the Crown Court.

Now test yourself

1 In which court would the following people be likely to be tried and why?

Defendant	Court
Fred has been charged with murder	
Sandra has been charged with stealing a large box of chocolates from the local supermarket	
Aaron has been charged with driving without insurance	
Kyle has been charged with stealing £60,000 from the elderly lady he was caring for	
Billy has pleaded guilty to causing actual bodily harm	

Answers on p.132

Bail

For any question on bail it is important to include the following information:

- Legislation
- Who can grant bail?
- Presumption in favour of bail
- Reasons for refusing bail
- Factors taken into account
- Unconditional and conditional bail
- Restrictions on granting bail
- Appeals.

Legislation

The Bail Act 1976 and subsequent amendments in the Bail (Amendment) Act 1993, the Crime and Disorder Act 1998, the Criminal Justice Act 2003 and the Coroners and Justice Act 2009 set out the legislation on bail.

Who can grant bail?

The police, magistrates and the Crown Court can all grant bail.

Presumption in favour of bail

There is a presumption that bail should be granted unless there is a good reason to refuse it.

Reasons for refusing bail

- Failure to surrender to custody
- Likely to commit further offences
- Interference with witnesses or the course of justice.

Factors to be taken into account

These include:

- the nature and seriousness of the offence
- the antecedents of the defendant
- any previous bail record
- the strength of evidence against the defendant.

Unconditional and conditional bail

Most commonly unconditional bail is granted. However, this does have one condition – that the suspect will attend court at the specified time.

Conditional bail

This is given if there are some risks in giving unconditional bail. The type of condition imposed will depend on the risk factors and can include:

- residence – at a bail hostel or their home address
- curfew with tagging
- handing in passport
- reporting at a police station at specified times
- exclusion zones
- contact bans
- Sureties.

Restrictions on granting bail

Although there is a presumption in favour of bail, it is rebutted in certain circumstances:

- For an offence committed while already on bail, bail can only be given if the court is satisfied there is no significant risk of further offending.
- Bail will only granted in exceptional circumstances for murder, attempted murder, manslaughter, rape or attempted rape if the defendant has already served a custodial sentence for such a crime.
- For murder, bail can only be granted by a judge at the Crown Court.
- Bail will be restricted for adult Class A drug users under the Criminal Justice Act 2003 in certain circumstances.
- The focus has recently changed from ensuring the right to liberty for the accused to ensuring the public is protected.

If no bail is granted, the suspect is remanded in custody.

Appeals

- The defendant must be taken before a Magistrates' Court at the first opportunity if the police refuse bail.
- Only one further application is allowed if bail is refused unless the circumstances have changed.
- An appeal may be made from a Magistrates' Court against refusal of bail to a judge in the Crown Court.
- The Bail Amendment Act 1993, as amended by the Criminal Justice Act 2003, gave the prosecution the right to appeal to a judge of the Crown Court against the granting of bail for any imprisonable offence.

Exam tip

Two or three examples of conditions are sufficient for any answer.

Typical mistake

A common mistake is to spend too long giving numerous examples of conditions and not explaining the reasons and factors taken into account when deciding whether or not to grant bail.

Points of discussion for part (b) questions in Section A

- It is difficult to get the balance right between protecting the public from potentially dangerous criminals and interfering with their liberty when there is a presumption of innocence before trial.
- There are over 8,000 prisoners on remand at any one time, which is extremely expensive.
- About 50% of those on remand are either found not guilty or given a non-custodial sentence. This implies they should have been given bail in the first place.

Exam practice answers and quick quizzes at **www.therevisionbutton.co.uk/myrevisionnotes**

- Thousands of people every year are having their liberty seriously interfered with, which suggests too many people are being remanded in custody.
- On the other side of the argument, there are also instances where people have committed violent crimes, including murder, whilst on bail. This also occurs whilst people are tagged and on a curfew, suggesting that some people given bail should have been remanded in custody.
- The Coroners and Justice Act 2009 has shifted the balance towards protecting the public. This may mean that fewer of those suspected of serious offences will be given bail in the future.

Now test yourself

Tested

2 Fill in the following grids.

Bail	
There is a presumption in favour of bail because...	
Reasons to refuse bail	**Why this is important**
1. D will fail to surrender to custody	
2. D will commit an offence whilst on bail	
3. D will interfere with witnesses or otherwise obstruct the course of justice	
4. D should be kept in custody for his/her own protection or welfare	

Factors to consider	Which reason to refuse does this relate to?	Examples
1. The nature and seriousness of the offence		
2. D's character, record, friends and community ties		
3. D's record of previous behaviour on bail		
4. The strength of evidence against D		

Consider the arguments for and against granting bail to each of the following cases. What conditions, if any, should be attached to bail if it is granted?

3 Elizabeth, aged 35, is a solicitor. She has a husband, three children and a comfortable home. Elizabeth is alleged to have defrauded one of her clients of several thousand pounds.

4 Brian, aged 25, has had a number of convictions for shoplifting in the last five years. He is currently charged with stealing a laptop worth £300 from a store. Brian lives in a caravan with his girlfriend. He is unemployed.

5 Bill, aged 23, has been charged with dealing in heroin. He was caught with a very considerable amount of heroin in the back of his car. He lives with his parents. Bill has worked as a plasterer for the same employer since he left school at 16 on an apprenticeship.

Answers on p.132

Typical mistake

(In Section B part b) questions.)

- Not using the name of the person in the scenario.
- There should be five distinct issues to identify and apply the law to. A common mistake is to only recognise some of them.
- Not concluding whether or not an issue will give D a better or worse chance of being granted bail.

Trial at first instance

Revised

A description of the trial process in either the Magistrates' Court or the Crown Court could be asked as part (a) of a question. Ensure that you know the correct order of events.

Now test yourself

Trial in the Magistrates' Court

6 Use the following statements to complete the flow chart in Figure 3.1.

a) Magistrates decide sentence.

b) Information needs to be gathered before sentencing.

c) Prosecution outlines the facts of the case.

d) Trial continues.

e) Defence witnesses are called.

f) Prosecution witnesses are called.

g) Prosecution witnesses cross-examined by the defence.

h) Defendant cross-examined by the prosecution.

i) CPS provides summary of the facts.

j) Defence argues mitigating factors.

k) Trial dismissed by magistrates.

l) Defence closes by summing up the prosecution case's weaknesses.

m) Not guilty: D is free to leave.

n) Defendant found guilty.

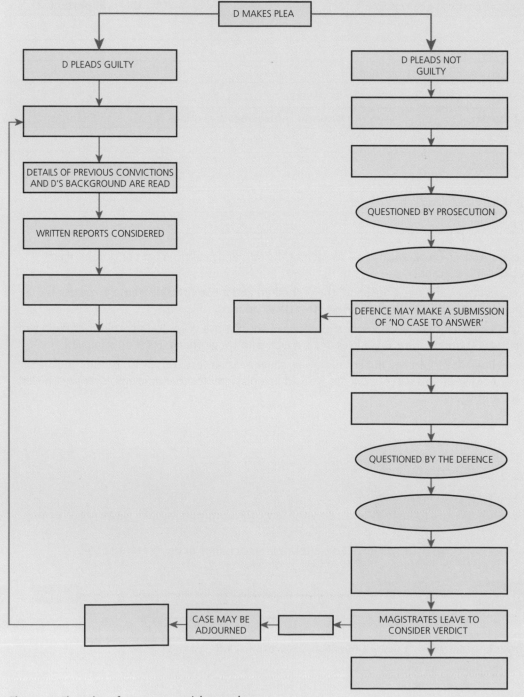

Figure 3.1 Flow chart for summary trial procedure

Exam practice answers and quick quizzes at **www.therevisionbutton.co.uk/myrevisionnotes**

Trial in the Crown Court

7 Use the following statements to complete the flow chart in Figure 3.2.

a) Prosecution closes.

b) Jury return and verdict is read out.

c) Crown Court judge decides sentence.

d) D submits plea at a plea and directions hearing.

e) Jury is sworn in.

f) Defence opens: set out their arguments.

g) Judge sums up and explains the law.

h) Jury retires to consider verdict.

i) Prosecution opens: summarise facts and their arguments.

j) Judge sentences D. May adjourn.

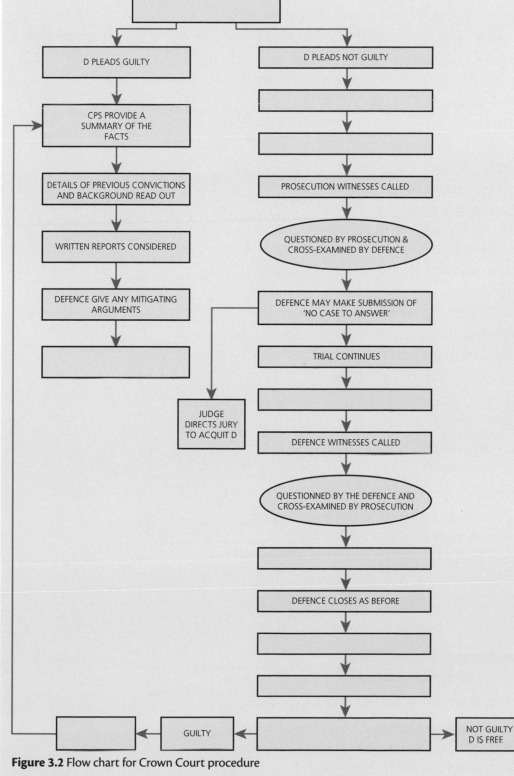

Figure 3.2 Flow chart for Crown Court procedure

Answers on pp.133–134

Appeals

Revised

It is important to learn the appeal routes from the Magistrates' Court and the Crown Court separately.

Appeal routes from the Magistrates' Court

Defence appeals to the Crown Court

- Defendant may appeal against conviction, sentence or both to the Crown Court if original plea was not guilty.
- Defendant may only appeal against sentence if original plea was guilty.
- No need for leave (permission) – there is an automatic right of appeal.
- The case will be completely re-heard by a judge and two magistrates.
- They may confirm conviction, reverse the decision and acquit the defendant or may vary the conviction and find the defendant guilty of a lesser offence.
- Sentence may be confirmed, increased (only to magistrates' maximum) or decreased.
- Out of about 12,000 appeals, half have some success.

Defence appeals by way of case stated to the Queen's Bench Divisional Court against conviction on a point of law

- Case stated = the facts are agreed beforehand and given as a statement to the court. The case is not re-heard in full.
- May be either directly from the Magistrates' Court or following appeal to the Crown Court.
- Only available for an appeal against conviction.
- Court may confirm, vary or reverse the decision or send the case back to the Magistrates' Court for them to apply the interpretation of the law.
- Only about 100 per year. An example is *C v DPP* (1996).

Prosecution appeal to the QBD against acquittal on a point of law only

- It is a case stated appeal.
- QBD can quash the decision, confirm it or send it back to the Magistrates' Court for a re-hearing.

Further appeal to the Supreme Court (House of Lords)

- Both the defence and prosecution can appeal further to the Supreme Court (from QBD) on a point of law of general public importance.
- Permission (leave) must be granted by the Supreme Court or Queen's Bench Division – it is rarely used.

It is acceptable in Part A of a question to use a diagram in your answer so long as the detail is there.

Appeal routes from the Crown Court

Revised

Appeals to the Court of Appeal

- Defendant may appeal against conviction, sentence or both to the Court of Appeal (Criminal Division). Leave to appeal must be granted either by the trial judge or from the Court of Appeal itself.

- Only ground for allowing an appeal against conviction is that the conviction is unsafe and the Court of Appeal may order a retrial or quash the conviction if it allows the defendant's appeal.
- When hearing an appeal, the Court of Appeal may admit new evidence in the interests of justice.
- The Criminal Cases Review Commission may refer cases back to the Court of Appeal after all routes of appeal have been exhausted if there is evidence of a miscarriage of justice.

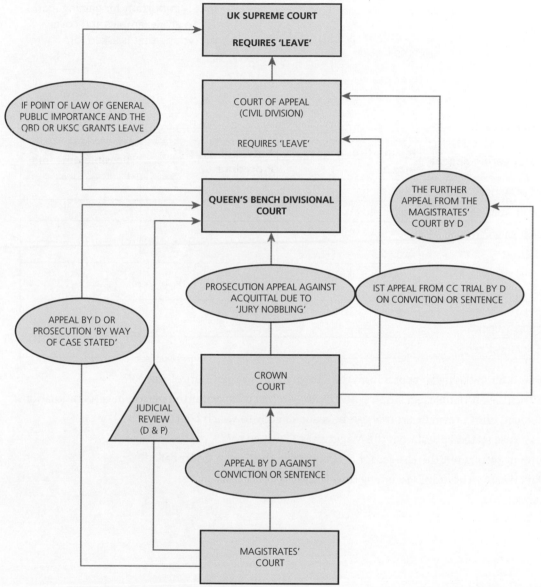

Figure 3.3 Appeal routes from the Crown Court

Challenges by the prosecution

- The prosecution may ask the Attorney-General to seek leave from the Court of Appeal to consider an unduly lenient sentence.
- The Attorney-General may refer a point of law to the Court of Appeal if the prosecution is concerned about an acquittal – this will merely settle the law on that point. It will not affect the acquittal.
- If there is evidence of jury tampering, the prosecution may apply to the High Court for the acquittal to be set aside and a retrial ordered.
- The Criminal Justice Act 2003 abolished the double jeopardy rule so that the Director of Public Prosecutions may apply to the Court of

Appeal to overturn an acquittal and order a retrial if there is new and compelling evidence.

- The prosecution may appeal against a ruling on law made by a judge in a Crown Court trial.

Appeals to the Supreme Court

- Both the prosecution and the defence have the right to appeal from the Court of Appeal (Criminal Division) to the Supreme Court. The Court of Appeal has to certify that it involves a point of law of public importance and either the Court of Appeal or the Supreme Court must give permission to appeal.
- Very few cases are appealed to the Supreme Court.

> **Exam tip**
>
> For part (a) of questions on any of these topics, it is the level of detail that is important for gaining marks. Try to give examples and cover everything that is asked for.

Now test yourself

Tested

8 Complete the following table:

Party	Court hearing appeal	Reason/Grounds for appeal	Nature of appeal/ Procedure	Possible outcome
Defendant	Court of Appeal	Conviction		
Defendant	Court of Appeal	Sentence		
Defendant	UK Supreme Court			
Prosecution	High Court	Acquittal		
Prosecution	Court of Appeal via Attorney-General	Acquittal (CJA 1972)		
Prosecution	Court of Appeal via Attorney-General	Sentence (s 36 CJA 1988)		
Prosecution	UK Supreme Court			

9 What is the time limit for initiating an appeal from the Crown Court to the Court of Appeal?

10 In which Act was the rule on 'double jeopardy' revised to allow retrial of an acquitted person in certain situations?

11 Appeals by the defence from Crown Court trial can be made directly to which court?

12 Which court does a case stated appeal from the Magistrates' Court go to?

13 What is the document setting out the charges for a defendant in the Crown Court called?

14 What happens directly after the judge's summing up in a Crown Court trial?

15 What does jurisdiction mean?

Answers on pp.134–135

4 Penal system

The knowledge required in this chapter relates to the following four areas:

The principles of sentencing:

1 The aims of sentencing

2 Factors taken into account when sentencing.

The powers of the courts:

3 Sentences available for adult offenders

4 Sentences available for young offenders.

Three main skills are needed:

● An ability to describe in detail the law relating to each area for part (a) questions in both sections of the paper.

● Development of analytical and critical points for Section A part (b), discussion questions.

● Application of relevant law for Section B part (b), scenario questions.

Principles of sentencing Revised ☐

The main aims of sentencing are set out in the Criminal Justice Act 2003.

Punishment

● Retribution for wrong-doing, society's revenge for the offence: 'Let the punishment fit the crime'. It is based on proportionality or 'just desserts'. The Sentencing Council produces guidelines on tariff sentences to reflect this aim.

● It also contains an element of denunciation – society's outrage at the offence committed.

Reduction of crime

● This includes both deterrence and rehabilitation.

Deterrence

Deterrence has two types – individual and general.

● **Individual** – this is aimed at a particular offender to put him/her off re-offending by either a very severe sentence, e.g. custodial sentence or a fine, or by the threat of imprisonment, e.g. a suspended sentence or conditional discharge.

● **General** – this is aimed at putting society off committing crimes by exemplary sentences or minimum sentences. These are not concerned with fairness and may be harsher than the usual tariff for the offence, so they can lead to injustice in particular cases, e.g. very severe sentences for the theft of mobile phones on the street.

Rehabilitation

This aims to reform the offender to stop them re-offending. It is focused on the longer term, looking at the potential of the offender to reform. It is now accepted that custodial sentences only have very limited rehabilitative effect and community orders are more likely to be used to achieve this aim.

Other elements of sentencing include the following:

Protection of the public

● Preventing the offender from re-offending. Curfews and custodial sentences may be used.

Reparation

● Considers the victim when sentencing the offender. Compensation orders are used to make the offender make amends to the victim.

Other factors that would be taken into account include:

● aggravating factors make the sentence more severe
● mitigating factors make the sentence more lenient
● the seriousness of the crime
● antecedents (previous records) of the offender, including any reports
● motive
● early guilty plea (this reduces the sentence by up to a third)
● sentencing guidelines/tariff.

Now test yourself

Tested ☐

1 Complete the following table with the appropriate names of the aims and the suitable punishments to fulfill those aims using the information given below.

Aim	Description of aim of theory	Suitable punishment
	Punishment imposed only on grounds that an offence has been committed, with no consideration of the defendant	
	The offender is deterred through fear of further punishment	
	Potential offenders warned as to likely punishment	
	Reform offender's behaviour	
	Offender is made incapable of committing further crime. Society is protected from crime	
	Repayment/reparation to victim or to community	
	Society expressing its disapproval. Reinforces moral boundaries	

Aims
Denunciation
Reparation
Rehabilitation
Individual deterrence
Retribution
General deterrence
Protection of the public

Sentences
Tariff sentences, sentence must be proportionate to the crime
Individualised sentence, community order
Long prison sentences, curfews with tagging, banning orders
Publicity, unpaid work, naming and shaming
Compensation order, unpaid work, reparation schemes
Long sentence as an example to others
Prison sentence, heavy fine

Answers on p.135

Powers of the courts

Sentences available for adults

Under the Criminal Justice Act (CJA) 2003 and the Crime and Disorder Act 1998, custodial sentences available for adults include:

- Mandatory life sentences, which is the only sentence available for murder if over 18 years old. Minimum term to be served before release on licence ranges from whole life to 15 years. Tariff set out in CJA 2003.
- Discretionary life sentences are available for other serious offences but the judge has discretion in imposing a lesser sentence if it is more appropriate.
- Fixed-term sentences where there is automatic release after half sentence is served. Only available if over 21 years old.
- Home Detention Curfew – early release from prison on a curfew.
- Indeterminate sentences for dangerous offenders for public protection.
- Extended sentences – custodial sentence up to the maximum for the crime followed by an extension period on licence.
- Minimum sentences for dealing in Class A drugs or a third burglary of a residential building.
- Suspended sentence of 28–51 weeks suspended for up to two years – sentence only has to be served if the offender commits further offences.

Community sentences for adults

- Generic 'Community Order' under the CJA 2003 which can include a range of 12 requirements for offenders over the age of 18. These can be mixed and matched.
- Unpaid Work Requirement – unpaid work in the community (40–300 hours).
- Supervision Requirement – the offender is put under the supervision of a probation officer.
- Drug Treatment and Testing Requirement.
- Curfew Requirement – for a certain number of hours a day the offender has to be in a specific place (may include electronic tagging).

Fines and other sentences for adults

- Fines unlimited in the Crown Court; £5,000 in the Magistrates' Court.
- Absolute and Conditional Discharges.
- Disqualification from driving.

Custodial sentences available for young offenders

- Detention at Her Majesty's Pleasure for murder if offender is 10–17 years old. An indeterminate sentence; the judge will recommend a minimum term.
- Young Offender's Institutions for offenders aged 18–20. This can be from 21 days up to the maximum for the offence. Offender will be transferred to adult prison if they turn 21 before release date.

- Detention and training orders for offenders aged 12–17 years, but only for persistent offenders. If aged under 15, the duration is from 4 to 24 months
- Detention for very serious crimes is available, allowing a young person to be detained for longer – up to the maximum for the offence.

Community sentences available for young offenders

The Youth Rehabilitation Order, brought in by the Criminal Justice and Immigration Act 2008, includes a range of 18 requirements that can be attached to it. This is similar to the Community Order but for 10–18 year olds. Some of these requirements are listed below:

- Activity requirement
- Attendance centre requirement
- Supervision requirement (supervision by local social services, a probation officer or a member of the Youth Offending Team)
- Unpaid work requirement only available if D is 16 years old or older on conviction
- A programme requirement
- An education requirement
- A local authority residence requirement
- Mental health treatment requirement
- Drug testing requirement.

Fines and other sentences

- Fines – will depend on the defendant's age: 10–13 years, maximum fine £250; 14–17 years, maximum fine £1,000; over 18, same as adult.
- ASBOs.
- Discharges, reprimands and warnings.

Now test yourself

Tested

2 Fill in the table with appropriate sentences available for each age range.

Age category	Custodial sentences	Community sentences	Fines	Discharges	Others
Under 12 (10–11)					
Under 14 (12–13)					
Under 16 (14–15)					
Under 18 (16–17)					
Under 21 (18–20)					
21+					

Answers on p.136

Advantages and disadvantages of the different types of sentence

Revised

Custodial sentences

Advantages

- Offenders cannot commit crimes when in prison so it protects the public.
- Opportunity to rehabilitate offenders.

Disadvantages

- Over 65% of ex-prisoners usually re-offend within two years and 80% of young offenders, so rehabilitation seems to be lacking.
- Prisoners can learn new ideas for committing crimes from other prisoners.
- Budget cuts and overcrowded prisons prevent any effective rehabilitation.
- The stigma of prison means opportunities to get employment after coming out is limited, pushing ex-offenders back into crime.
- There is family breakdown and many ex-prisoners become homeless.
- Prison is very expensive – three weeks in prison costs more than a whole year of a community order.
- Many people who should not be in prison are put there – e.g. for non-payment of fines or council tax. Non-violent offenders, asylum seekers and people on remand could be dealt with more effectively and cheaply in the community.
- Most other European countries only have a third of our prison population in proportion to their total population.
- Conditions in prison are poor and suicide rates are high.
- Sir David Ramsbotham, who was Chief Inspector of Prisons, claimed that the prison population could be cut in half if you took away young people, the elderly, the mentally ill, asylum seekers and those inside for trivial shoplifting and drug offences.

Community sentences

Advantages

- Less disruptive than custody as offender keeps living with family and can continue job.
- Most offenders given supervision orders find them useful as it allows them to talk through their problems and confront their behaviour.
- Much cheaper than custody.
- Unpaid work gives offenders a sense of achievement.
- Tagging is effective at keeping offenders out of trouble and protecting the public, is much cheaper than prison and, as the technology improves, should remove the need for imprisonment for many offenders.

Disadvantages

- Tagging can be seen as degrading to the offender – though is less degrading than imprisonment.
- Re-offending rates are still quite high.
- Crime prevention is more likely to lower crime rates than any type of sentence, as offenders never think they will get caught.

Fines

Advantages

- Brings in revenue to the courts.
- A quick penalty for minor crime.
- Linked to ability to pay.

Disadvantages

- Problems collecting fines – magistrates do not always use their powers to collect fines from pay or benefits and send people to prison for non-payment.
- Under the Criminal Justice Act 2003, a person can do unpaid work to pay off a fine at £6 per hour but supervising this is also expensive.

Typical mistake

- Not reading the question properly.
- Confusing aims of sentencing with types of sentence.
- Only concentrating on one type of sentence, e.g. custodial or community – a range is necessary for high marks, if that is asked for.
- Getting the sentences available for young offenders and adult offenders confused.
- Only answering half the question.
- Answering a different question to the one asked.
- Lack of detail.

Exam tip

Answering part (a) of a question on sentencing

- ✔ Read the question carefully.
- ✔ Ensure you are clear on the difference between aims of sentencing and sentences available.
- ✔ Ensure you put in some detail (do not make lists without detail).
- ✔ If the question is generally about types of sentence, ensure you describe some sentences from all four types, i.e. custodial, community, fines and other sentences.
- ✔ If the question is more specific, only describe the types of sentence asked for. If you are asked to describe custodial and community sentences for adults, do not waste time on fines or discharges.
- ✔ If the question asks for a description of the aims of sentencing, describe all the main aims and if factors are required, be sure to explain the main factors.

How to answer scenario questions

- Refer to the subject of the scenario throughout your answer.
- A scenario will usually give one offender convicted of a crime and ask you to discuss what would be taken into account in deciding the sentence.
- You should apply the aims of sentencing systematically and say why some would be more important than others. You should also discuss what other factors might be taken into account and suggest a possible sentence or sentences.
- There are usually at least five issues to identify in the scenario – make sure you identify them and apply the relevant law with reasons.
- Come to a conclusion for each issue.

5 The judiciary

Judges

The knowledge required in this chapter relates to the following areas:

- Selection and appointment of judges
- What training do they receive?
- What is the role of the judge in each of the different courts, i.e. Crown Court, civil courts of first instance and appeal courts?
- What sorts of background do judges have?
- Is the new appointments procedure likely to give a better cross-section of society?
- What sort of tenure do judges have?
- How does the theory of the separation of powers work and how does it apply to judges?
- Are judges independent?
- Should we have a career judiciary like in France?

Two main skills are needed:

- An ability to describe in detail the law relating to each area for part (a) questions in both sections of the paper.
- Development of analytical and critical points for Section A part (b), discussion questions.

What are the qualifications required for each level of judicial appointment?

- Set out in the Tribunals, Court and Enforcement Act 2007.
- Justices of the Supreme Court – hold high judicial office or have held superior court qualification for at least 15 years – can be from Northern Ireland or Scotland as well as England and Wales.
- Lords Justices of Appeal – existing High Court judge or at least seven years' qualification.
- High Court judges – barrister or solicitor for seven years or Circuit Judge for two years.
- Circuit Judge – barrister or solicitor for seven years, Recorder, District Judge or Tribunal Judge.
- Recorder – barrister or solicitor for seven years.
- District Judge – barrister or solicitor for five years or ILEX fellow (deputy District Judge first).

How are judges selected?

- Supreme Court judges are selected like all other judges. Selection is organised by the Judicial Appointments Commission.
- Selection by a mixed panel of judges, lay people and lawyers.
- All appointments now advertised.
- The aim is to diversify the judiciary.
- Candidates apply and provide references.
- There are interviews to assess attitude and aptitude.
- The Lord Chancellor has a limited power to object to selection.
- Applicants for higher appointments are expected to show competence at a lower level (appointment at assistant recorder level is usually used to try out potential judges for more permanent positions).

> **Exam tip**
>
> Ensure that you know the difference between qualifications and selection. Qualifications are the legal qualifications and experience required before a person can even be considered for a job. Selection is the process whereby those qualified who apply for the post are chosen.

How are judges trained?

- Training conducted by the Judicial Studies Board.
- For superior judges, training is voluntary.
- For an inferior judge, training is compulsory – mainly for newly appointed assistant recorders and consists of a one-week course which deals with sentencing, running a criminal court and human awareness.
- Inferior judges also have to spend a week shadowing an experienced judge before sitting themselves.
- One-day courses are run from time to time to update judges on major changes in the law, some of which are compulsory, e.g. Human Rights Act 1998.

What is the role of judges at first instance?

In all courts:

- To ensure the hearing is carried out fairly and preside over the court
- To decide questions of law.

In criminal cases:

- Magistrates' Court – decide both verdict and sentence and preliminary, matters e.g. bail
- Crown Court – sum up for jury, sentence if appropriate.

In civil cases:

- Decisions made by a single judge
- Decide verdict and award; in small claims help parties put their case
- Act as case manager, deciding track, holding preliminary hearings to clarify issues, keep parties to time limits, may be responsible for running court office.

What is the role of judges in the appeal courts?

Revised

- Review the hearing at first instance; decide whether the law was correctly decided and whether hearing carried out properly.
- Decisions are made by three or more judges sitting together.
- Decide whether result is wrong or unsafe.
- Can change decision or may order a retrial.
- Can revise sentence or award.
- Can decide issues of law in important cases (UK Supreme Court and Court of Appeal usually).
- Can clarify or amend the law where appropriate (*R v G & R*).
- May be involved in judicial review in the Divisional High Court.
- May be reviewing situations in relation to the Human Rights Act 1998.

Background of judges

Revised

Before the changes in appointment:

- Were originally only appointed from the ranks of barristers and appointed on recommendation of Lord Chancellor with secret soundings
- There were still very few women or ethnic minorities
- Supreme Court Judges – over 80% went to public school and Oxbridge and came from wealthy backgrounds.

Since the changes in appointment:

- Appointments from applications and based on merit
- All vacancies advertised and require applications
- Positive steps to diversify the judiciary – more women and ethnic minorities being encouraged to apply
- Promotions from current inferior judges to the more senior positions
- The Judicial Appointments Commission should lead to greater diversity
- More women and people from ethnic minorities are now being appointed, but is at the lower ranks of judges
- It will take many years to diversify the judiciary to any great extent.

Tenure of judges

Revised

- Senior judges have security of tenure under the Act of Settlement 1701 and cannot be removed except by the Monarch following a petition to both Houses of Parliament.
- Superior judges can be asked to resign.
- Inferior judges can be removed by the Lord Chancellor and the Lord Chief Justice for incapacity or misbehaviour but must comply with set procedures (Constitutional Reform Act 2005).
- Recorders are only appointed for a period of five years but must be reappointed unless there is a good reason.
- Judges retire at 70.

Now test yourself

1 Fill in the following grid detailing the role of judges in various courts.

Type of judge	How many are there?	Which court/courts do they sit in?	What is their role?
Justices of the Supreme Court			
Lords Justices of Appeal			
High Court Judges			
Circuit Judges			
Recorders			
District Judges			
District Judges (Magistrates' Court)			

Answer the following questions.

2 Which body is responsible for the training of judges?

3 At what age are inferior judges meant to retire?

4 Which Act of Parliament contains the most recent changes to required judicial qualifications?

5 In what year did the first all-female Court of Appeal panel sit?

6 What year was the Supreme Court established?

7 What is the role of the Supreme Court?

8 When was racial awareness training introduced for judges?

9 In what year was the first woman appointed to the Court of Appeal?

Answers on pp.136–137

How to answer a Section A question on the judiciary

1 Describe the qualifications, selection and training of judges.

OCR Specimen paper

First **plan** your answer

This sort of question has several parts and you need to ensure you answer each of the three parts to the question. Start with describing the qualifications required, then go on to the process of selection and follow this with the training. You are only giving information – you do not need to comment in Section A part (a) questions.

The qualifications required before a judge can be appointed to a particular level are set out in the Tribunals, Court and Enforcement Act 2007. Justices of the Supreme Court are appointed from those that hold high judicial office or have 15 years' qualification for appearance in the senior courts in England and Wales or Scotland and Northern Ireland. They are selected by a Supreme Court Selection Committee specially convened by the Lord Chancellor when a vacancy arises. Lords Justices of Appeal must be an existing High Court judge or have been a barrister or solicitor for at least seven years. High Court judges must have spent two years as a Circuit Judge or have been a barrister or solicitor for seven years. A Circuit Judge may have been a Recorder, District Judge or a Tribunal Chair or been a barrister or solicitor for seven years.

Recorders must have seven years' experience as a barrister or solicitor and District Judges need to have had five years' such experience.

Apart from the Supreme Court judges, all other judicial selection is organised by the Judicial Appointments Commission. Selection is by a mixed panel of judges, lay people and lawyers. All appointments are now advertised with the aim to diversify the judiciary. Potential judges must apply and provide references. They are interviewed to assess attitude and aptitude. The Lord Chancellor has a very limited power to object to selection. Applicants for higher appointments are expected to show competence at a lower level; appointment at assistant recorder level is usually used to try out potential judges for more permanent positions.

Training is conducted by the Judicial Studies Board, and for superior judges the training is still voluntary. For an inferior judge, training is compulsory – mainly for newly appointed assistant recorders, and consists of a one-week course which deals with sentencing, running a criminal court and human awareness.

Inferior judges also have to spend a week shadowing an experienced judge before sitting themselves.

One-day courses are run from time to time to update judges on major changes in the law, some of which are compulsory, e.g. Human Rights Act 1998.

How to answer a part (b) discussion question

1 Discuss the way in which judicial independence is maintained.

OCR Specimen paper

The main thing to consider with part b) questions is that you need to provide at least three well-developed points of discussion that are directly answering the question.

Judicial independence is maintained in many ways. A judge cannot be sued for what is said or done in court (**point**) which gives the judge freedom to come to an unpopular decision (**development**); however they can still be criticised in the appeal courts (**further development to make it a well-developed point**).

By convention to keep the judiciary free of politics (**point**): full-time judges cannot become MPs and should avoid making political comments (**development**). Supreme Court Justices no longer sit in the House of Lords as law makers and have been provided with a new building away from Parliament to further distance them from the legislature (**well developed**).

Judges do sometimes have to take decisions that have a political element, in particular judicial review (**point**) but demonstrate their independence by sometimes declaring delegated legislation *ultra vires* (**development**).

The appointment of judges now leads to better independence as they are independently appointed on merit on past record (**point**), with tests and references but there is a political element for superior judges despite reforms (**development**).

Judges have secure tenure as a motion of Parliament is needed to remove superior judges (**point**) and good reason is needed for inferior judges. Even Recorders' contracts must be renewed except for good reason (**development**); however any judge can be eased out by not having any work allocated to them (**well developed**).

The separation of powers Revised

The three arms of the state:

- **Legislature:** makes law – Parliament and the Queen
- **Executive:** puts laws into effect and administers nation's affairs – Ministers (and their departments)
- **Judiciary:** interpret and enforce law – judges.

The three arms must be kept independent of each other. This means that each can exercise control over the other two. Without this separation, it is easier for one person or a small group to take complete control (e.g. Zimbabwe).

This gives some independence to the judiciary:

- By giving security of tenure to the judiciary (in the Act of Settlement)

- But judges do try to implement intention of Parliament in Statutory Interpretation
- Judges cannot question legality of legislation.

Controls are exercised by:

- the judiciary providing a check on executive through judicial review
- the executive providing a check on the higher judiciary
- judiciary can be thought to limit legislature through statutory interpretation, e.g. the golden rule – judges may decide a literal interpretation would lead to an absurd or obnoxious result and give a different interpretation
- legislature has some control over the terms of judges' employment, e.g. pay, retirement age
- the legislature can amend a law if a minister has been held to be acting *ultra vires*.

How is judicial independence maintained?

- Judges cannot be sued for what is said or done in court which gives a judge freedom to come to an unpopular decision but this can be criticised in the appeal courts.
- By convention judges keep free of politics: cannot become MPs (except for Recorders), avoid making political comments, Law Lords can only take part in relevant debates – but LCJ and MR have felt the need to publicly voice concerns about issues such as sentencing.
- Judges do sometimes have to take decisions that have a political element, e.g. judicial review.
- Independently appointed on merit on past record, tests and references but there is a political element for superior judges despite reforms.
- Secure tenure – need a motion of Parliament to remove superior judges and good reason for inferior judges. Recorders' contracts must be renewed except for good reason but can be eased out.
- Financially secure – salary set independently, have pension provision but this is now comparatively low in level as judges have to work 20 years to gain full pension.
- Judges must not have any personal interest in a case they are hearing – *Pinochet* case.
- Judicial Appointments Commission should lead to more independence.

Should we have a career judiciary?

Advantages

- Judges will be younger as they will not have worked as an advocate first.
- Will have trained for longer in judicial skills – at present there is minimal training on human awareness, sentencing and presiding over a criminal court.
- Greater scope for specialisation.
- Able to concentrate on decision-making skills.
- Selected for judicial skills – not all good advocates become good judges.

Disadvantages

- Being younger may not be an advantage as judges will lack life experience.
- Less experience of court practice and barristers' techniques.
- Less experience of dealing with clients and possibly human awareness.
- Loss of advocate's habit of independence.

Now test yourself

Tested

10 Try to complete the diagram below on the separation of powers.

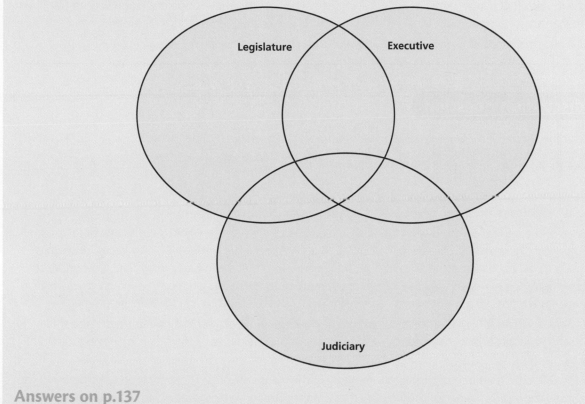

Legislature Executive

Judiciary

Answers on p.137

How to answer a question on the separation of powers

1 Describe the theory of the separation of powers using examples to illustrate your answer. **[18 marks]**

OCR G141 June 2008

The main thing to consider with such a question is to remember this is a law paper not a politics paper, so it is important to stick to the issues concerned.

The theory of the separation of powers was put forward by the French political theorist Montesquieu. The theory is based on the fact that in a democracy the three arms of the state, the legislature, the executive and the judiciary, should be kept separate from each other in order to prevent too much power being vested in a person or group of people. Some countries such as the USA incorporate the separation of powers in their constitution to prevent any overlap.

In this country the legislature, which in this case is Parliament, makes the law.

The executive puts those laws into effect and administers the countries' affairs. This consists of the government, i.e. ministers and their departments.

The judiciary interprets and enforces the law.

Ideally, they should be kept separate but there are some overlaps, especially between the executive and the legislature as the government dominates the choice of legislation passing through Parliament and with a good majority can force much legislation through.

There was more overlap in the past with the role of the Lord Chancellor which covered all three arms of the state as he was the equivalent of the Speaker in the House of Lords controlling that part of the legislature, he was in charge of a government department which was responsible for the selection of judges, and he sat as a judge. This has been reformed and he is now not a judge in the Supreme Court nor does he have a large role in the selection of Judges. House of Lords judges used to also have a role in legislation but judges of the new Supreme Court do not.

The theory does, however, work to an extent as the judiciary enjoys some independence from the legislature and the executive. They enjoy security of tenure. Although they cannot question primary legislation and they should try to implement the intention of Parliament through statutory interpretation, they have some discretion with the various approaches to statutory interpretation. They can also check on the executive through judicial review.

Parliament also has some control over the executive as they can amend the law if a minister acts *ultra vires*.

Another discussion question

1 Discuss why the theory of the separation of powers is important to judicial independence.   **[12 marks]**

OCR G141 June 2008

For a part b) discussion question, remember you have to provide at least three well-developed points to get full marks. Try to identify where the point, development and further development come in the following answer.

The importance of the separation of powers to judicial independence has been recognised and is one of the reasons for many of the recent reforms into the selection of the judiciary. When judges were selected by 'secret soundings' it was very much a political decision and any judge seeking promotion could be influenced by that. Now under the Judicial Appointments Commission, their selection is much more transparent and on merit, which prevents political influence except for the limited power the Lord Chancellor still retains to object to a judge being appointed.

The reforms to the role of the Lord Chancellor mean that he no longer holds power in all three arms of the state. He no longer sits as a judge, or is involved to any great extent with the selection of judges. This improves judicial independence.

The Law Lords used to be members of the legislature sitting in the House of Lords. The separation of powers was seen as so important to the independence of the judiciary that it was necessary to build a new and separate court for the new Supreme Court and these judges would no longer sit in the House of Lords.

Typical mistake

- Lack of knowledge or out-of-date knowledge on selection and appointment.
- Lack of knowledge on training.
- Roles of judges in civil and criminal courts are often mixed up.
- Lack of examples of judicial independence.

How to avoid these mistakes

- Ensure you know the different roles of judges in criminal and civil cases.
- Learn how judges are appointed and trained.
- Ensure you understand the theory of the separation of powers and how the new reforms have had an impact on how it functions.

6 The legal profession

For the purposes of the OCR AS Law course, you are required to have detailed knowledge of the following:

- Solicitors
- Barristers.

Both these professions can be broken down into four distinct AO1 areas:

- Education and training
- Work
- Organisation
- Regulation.

The main skills needed are:

- Ability to describe, in detail, each of the above four elements.
- Ability to analyse central issues and develop clear arguments.

Solicitors
Revised ☐

A solicitor is a lawyer who deals directly with clients by giving legal advice, preparing legal documents and, if necessary, representing a client in court. A firm of solicitors can be found in most towns and cities and it is from these professionals that a person will usually seek initial advice on a legal matter.

Education and training
Revised ☐

Academic stage – education

The quickest route to becoming a solicitor is to complete a Solicitors Regulation Authority (SRA)-approved qualifying law degree containing compulsory foundation/core topics, for example, legal research, obligations, public and criminal law. There will also be option modules, for example, environmental law, intellectual property, and consumer law.

If a person has a degree in another subject, they are required to undertake an additional training course, the Common Professional Examination (CPE) or the Graduate Diploma in Law (GDL). This course covers the foundation/core topics as stated above. Before continuing with training, student membership of the SRA must be applied for.

Vocational training – Legal Practice Course (LPC)

The next stage is the LPC which develops the skills required to practice as a solicitor. It is practical-based, with emphasis on skills such as client-interviewing, negotiation, drafting documents, business management and advocacy. The course is either one year full time or two years part time. The average cost of the LPC is £12,000.

> **Exam tip**
> It is possible to get full marks for education and training by drawing a diagram; however the diagram must contain detailed descriptions.

> **Exam tip**
> In order to obtain maximum marks for this part, you are required to do more than simply state a degree is necessary. Make sure you describe the education and training and give examples of foundation/core elements of the degree.

> **Exam tip**
> In order to obtain maximum marks for this part, it is necessary to do more than simply name the course. Make sure you describe the course in detail, giving examples of what the course covers.

Professional/practical training – training contract

The final stage of the training is a two-year training contract with a firm of solicitors or an organisation authorised by the SRA to take trainees. The trainee must gain experience in at least three different areas of English law. During this time a student will be paid a minimum of £16,650 per annum.

The Professional Skills Course

During the training contract, the trainee must attend and satisfactorily complete the Professional Skills Course. This course builds on the vocational training provided by the LPC.

Admission to the Roll

Upon successful completion of all the above, the person is now a qualified solicitor and admitted to the Roll of Solicitors and able to apply for a practising certificate.

> **Exam tip**
>
> As before, in order to obtain maximum marks for this part, it is necessary to do more than simply name the course. Make sure you describe the course in detail, giving examples of what the course covers.

Check your understanding

1 Identify three of the qualifying law degree/CPE/GDL core/foundation subjects.
2 Describe the Legal Practice Course.
3 Identify three different areas of English law a trainee solicitor may cover during their training contract.
4 Describe in outline the Professional Skills Course.
5 Identify when a trainee solicitor is admitted to the Roll of Solicitors.

Answers on p.137

Work

Revised ☐

Solicitors undertake a wide range of work. They provide legal advice to clients and represent their clients in court. The majority of solicitors work in private practice. There are other career options open to a qualified solicitor, for example, working for the Crown Prosecution Service, local or national government or working for a legal department of a commercial or industrial business.

Solicitors may undertake the following work:

- Meeting with clients and taking instructions and offering advice
- Drafting legal documents
- Conveyancing, which is the transfer of legal title of property from one person to another, for example, buying or selling a residential property
- Wills and probate – dealing with the estate of a deceased person
- Matrimonial and family matters, for example, divorce and child custody
- Negligence, for example, personal injury claims
- Negotiating on behalf of their clients
- Advocacy – all solicitors have rights of audience in the lower courts. Under the Solicitors' Higher Rights of Audience Regulations 2010, a solicitor, once admitted to the Roll, can apply for the higher courts qualification. There is no longer an experience or mandatory training requirement. All solicitors must demonstrate the required practical advocacy skills and, as a minimum, have passed the advocacy module of the LPC. The solicitor will be required to sit and pass assessments.

Organisation

Revised

- Solicitors are represented by the Law Society and controlled by the Solicitors Regulation Authority.
- Solicitors can work for small or large firms and can be sole practitioners or in a partnership.
- The Legal Services Act 2007 now allows both Legal Disciplinary Practices and Alternative Business Structures. Solicitors can form companies rather than partnerships and the company does not need to be owned by solicitors.

Regulation

Revised

Solicitors deal directly with their clients and a contract is formed between them, allowing both parties to sue for breach of contract. The solicitor can sue for non-payment of fees and the client for failure of the solicitor to, for example, complete work to a satisfactory standard. Both *Griffiths v Dawson* (1993) and *White v Jones* (1995) demonstrate where the solicitor provided a less than satisfactory standard of work. In *Hall v Simons* (2000), the House of Lords decided that advocates can be liable for negligent advocacy.

An unsatisfied client must first utilise the solicitor's firm's complaints procedure. If the outcome is not satisfactory, the complaint will be dealt with by the Office for Legal Complaints set up by the Legal Services Act 2007. All complaints are referred to the Legal Ombudsman. The Legal Ombudsman has the power to ask the solicitor to apologise to the client, give back any documents the client might need, put things right if more work can correct what went wrong, refund or reduce the legal fees, or pay compensation of up to £30,000.

The Solicitors Regulation Authority regulates the profession of solicitors and will investigate any alleged professional misconduct of solicitors. If there is evidence of serious misconduct, the case will be put before the Solicitors Disciplinary Tribunal who can fine, reprimand, suspend or strike off the solicitor from the Roll.

Barristers

Revised

Barristers are specially trained to advise clients on the strengths and weaknesses of their case and to act as court room advocates.

Education and training

Revised

Academic stage – education

The quickest route to becoming a barrister is to complete a Bar Standards Board-approved qualifying law degree. This degree will contain compulsory foundation/core topics, for example, legal research, obligations, public and criminal law. There will also be option modules, for example, environmental law, intellectual property and consumer law.

If a person has a degree in another subject they are required to undertake an additional training course, the Common Professional Examination (CPE) or the Graduate Diploma in Law (GDL). This course covers the foundation/core topics as stated above.

> **Exam tip**
>
> In order to obtain maximum marks for this part, you are required to do more than simply state a degree is necessary. Make sure you describe the education and training and give examples of foundation/core elements of the degree.

Membership of an Inn of Court

Before continuing with training, membership of one of the four Inns of Court must be obtained. The four Inns are Inner Temple, Middle Temple, Gray's Inn and Lincoln's Inn. A student is expected to undertake 12 qualifying sessions at their chosen Inn or attend residential training courses during the Bar Professional Training Course.

Exam tip

For maximum marks, it is essential to remember a student joins the Inn of Court **before** they start the BPTC.

Vocational training – Bar Professional Training Course (BPTC)

This course can either be taken over one year full time or two years part time. The BPTC develops the skills required for a career at the Bar. It is practically based and includes advocacy and role-playing, case preparation, drafting legal documents, opinion-writing (giving written advice on cases) and interpersonal skills. Fees for the BPTC vary between £9,500 and £15,750 for the year.

Exam tip

In order to obtain maximum marks for this part, it is necessary to do more than simply name the course. Make sure you describe the course in detail, giving examples of what the course covers.

Admission to the Bar

Upon completion of the BPTC, a student is eligible to be 'Called to the Bar'. This is a graduation ceremony held at the chosen Inn of Court. Once 'Called', the student is officially qualified and has the title 'barrister'; however, if they wish to practise or call themself a barrister in connection with the supply of legal services, they must complete a final stage of training.

Exam tip

For maximum marks, it is essential to remember that it is after the BPTC and before pupillage that a student is Called to the Bar.

Professional/practical training – pupillage

The final stage of the training process is a one-year pupillage which is similar to an apprenticeship. The trainee becomes a pupil to a qualified barrister (Pupil Supervisor) and this is usually undertaken at a set of chambers. Pupillage is divided into two parts or 'sixes', the 'first six' is non-practising and entails shadowing the Supervisor. During the 'second six' the pupil is able to undertake supervised work of their own. During this time the student will be paid a minimum of £12,000 for the year.

Exam tip

As before, in order to obtain maximum marks for this part, it is necessary to do more than simply state 'pupillage must be undertaken'. Make sure you describe the process in detail.

Check your understanding

6 Identify when a trainee barrister joins one of the Inns of Court.

7 Describe three elements of the BPTC.

8 Describe the two 'sixes' of pupillage.

9 Identify when a barrister is Called to the Bar.

10 Identify what a barrister is able to do upon completion of pupillage.

Answers on p.137

Work

Revised

The majority of barristers are self-employed (approximately 80%) and concentrate on advocacy, although some barristers specialise in areas which rarely require attendance at court, for example, tax law. The remainder are employed by, for example, central or local government and industry and advise the organisation for which they work.

Barristers may undertake the following work:

● Advocacy – representing clients in court. The barrister will present the case, examining and cross-examining witnesses and sum up all relevant material

● Legal research

- Holding case conferences with clients and advising them on the law and the strength of their legal case
- Writing 'an opinion' for the client
- Negotiating settlements with the other side.

Organisation

Revised

- Barristers are controlled by the General Council of the Bar and they must be a member of one of the four Inns of Court.
- Self-employed barristers gain 'tenancy' and work from a set of shared 'chambers'. A Practice Administrator and other administrative staff will manage the work coming into the chambers and negotiate the fee to be paid.
- Self-employed barristers usually work on instruction from a solicitor but there is Direct Access in civil cases where anyone can go directly to a barrister without having to involve anyone else.
- Some barristers operate the Cab-rank rule whereby they have to accept any work if it is on the area of law they deal with and are free to take the case. The rule is not applicable in Direct Access cases.
- After 10 years of practising as a barrister, it is possible to become a Queen's Counsel and 'Take Silk'.

Regulation

Revised

There is no contract between the client and the barrister except in situations of Direct Access, and as a result, the client cannot sue for breach of contract. However, the client can sue for negligence regarding written advice (Saif Ali v Sydney Mitchell and Co (1980)) and negligent advocacy in court (Hall v Simmons (2000)).

An unsatisfied client will first use the Chamber's In-House Complaints Procedure. If the outcome is not satisfactory, the complaint will be dealt with by the Office for Legal Complaints set up by the Legal Services Act 2007. All complaints are referred to the Legal Ombudsman. The Legal Ombudsman has the power to ask the barrister to apologise to the client, give back any documents the client might need, put things right if more work can correct what went wrong, refund or reduce the legal fees, or pay compensation of up to £30,000.

The Bar Standards Board regulates the profession of barristers and will investigate any alleged breach of the Code of Conduct. It can discipline any barrister who is in breach and if the matter is serious, it will be referred to the Disciplinary Tribunal of the Council of the Inns of Court

Assessment of both solicitors and barristers – AO2

Revised

There is little doubt that the two professions are merging closer and closer and the differences between them have significantly reduced. The introduction of Direct Access for barristers and the Solicitors' Higher Rights of Audience Regulations 2010 mean that there is little difference between the two professions. The Legal Services Act 2007 now allows the two professions to work together.

In terms of complaints, the Legal Services Act 2007 took away the complaints mechanism from the professions' governing bodies, i.e. the Law Society and the Bar Council and set up an independent complaints department. It is hoped that the Office for Legal Complaints and the Legal Ombudsman will stop the considerable delays in dealing with complaints and simplify the system. The increase in powers given to the Ombudsman ensures those who complain are more likely to get an impartial and just decision, including a reasonable amount of compensation.

There are, however, still major criticisms of the training process of both solicitors and barristers. Some of the key criticisms are:

- The cost of undertaking the education and vocational training may put off many able candidates, particularly with fees for university degrees having increased. Although there are student loans available for the degree, the LPC is a post-graduate course and as a result, there is no funding available. There are bursaries available to help with costs of training, more so for trainee barristers. The effect of the financial difficulties is that it may lead to only those with financial backing being able to qualify and these may not necessarily be the best people. For those wishing to become a solicitor, it is possible to undertake the ILEX route, which means the student is being paid whilst training; however there is no such route for would-be barristers.

- There is much criticism of the CPE/GDL as it is said, by some, to not give sufficient grounding in law when compared to the rigours of a qualifying law degree. Both the Bar Council and the Law Society, in a joint statement, stated that '18 months should be spent on the core subjects' and the CPE/GDL courses last only one year. However, it is an opportunity for candidates with other degrees to enter the profession later and these candidates bring different skills with them.

- The choice to become a barrister or solicitor has to be made upon the completion of the law degree of CPE/GDL without any vocational or practical training being undertaken. Some say that this is far too early to make an informed choice.

- There are great difficulties in finding a pupillage/training contract and as a result, many are prevented from completing their training. Approximately only one in five trainees Called to the Bar are able to obtain pupillage. There is also said to be a training-contract 'lottery', with up to 70 applicants per job. A great deal of time and money has been spent getting so far only to find you are unable to achieve your goal. The quality of pupillage/training contracts also varies in terms of actual work and support.

- Even after completing all the various training elements there is still an over-supply of qualified lawyers – far too many qualify for the jobs available.

> **Typical mistake**
>
> - Getting the training muddled up between barristers and solicitors.
> - Not getting the training in the right order, in particular when a barrister is Called to the Bar.
> - Lack of detail on all aspects.
> - Only talking about costs when considering the problems of training.
> - Not answering the question asked – if the question is about work and complaints, training is irrelevant.

Now test yourself

1 Using the following table, compare the training of solicitors and barristers.

Training	Solicitors	Barristers
Education – academic		
Vocational training		
Practical stage		

Answers on p.137

Exam practice

a) Describe the education and training of solicitors and the different types of work which they undertake. **[18 marks]**

b) Discuss whether the lack of availability of training contracts is the main problem with the education and training of solicitors. **[12 marks]**

OCR G151 January 2012

Answers and quick quizzes online

Online

Student activity

Consider the training of the legal professions

Produce three arguments to support how the training of barristers and solicitors is carried out and three arguments to illustrate the problems. Each point needs to be developed and then developed further.

Good points about the training:

1

2

3

Problems with the training:

1

2

3

Answers on p.138

7 Lay people in the legal system

Lay people have been involved in the English legal system for over 800 years. They uphold the important principle in our legal system of trial by one's peers. Using lay people in the justice system allows ordinary men and women to participate in the administration of justice.

For the purposes of the OCR AS Law course, you are required to have detailed knowledge of the following:

- Lay magistrates (lay justices); and
- Juries.

Exam tip

An examination question may ask you to look at lay magistrates and/ or juries or it may ask you to discuss both together under the heading of lay people.

Lay magistrates (lay justices)   Revised

This topic can be broken down into five distinct areas:

- Formal requirements, disqualifications and qualities
- Selection and appointment
- Training
- Work/role
- Evaluation, including advantages and disadvantages.

Two main skills are needed:

- Ability to describe, in detail, each of the above five elements.
- Ability to analyse central issues and develop clear arguments.

Formal requirements, disqualifications and qualities   Revised

Formal requirements

There are no formal legal qualifications required to become a member of the magistracy; however, a person must fulfil the following three formal requirements:

1 Be aged between 18 and 65 on appointment
2 Live or work near the Local Justice Area they are allocated to
3 Be prepared to commit to sitting at least 26 half days per year.

Disqualifications

The Lord Chancellor and Secretary of State for Justice will not appoint certain people. Some examples of those not eligible or disqualified are:

- those with serious previous convictions or a number of minor offences
- undischarged bankrupts
- a serving police officer
- traffic wardens
- full-time members of the Armed Forces
- anyone whose work or community activity is incompatible with the duties of a magistrate, e.g. CPS or probation employee.

Exam tip

To demonstrate good understanding, explain why one or two or the above are disqualified or not eligible to become a lay magistrate.

Qualities

If a person fulfils the above, there are six qualities which a candidate must have. These were set by the Lord Chancellor in 1998 and are:

- maturity and sound temperament
- commitment and reliability
- good character
- understanding and communication
- social awareness
- sound judgement.

Exam tip

To demonstrate good understanding, describe/explain in more detail one or two of the above qualities.

Selection and appointment

Revised

A person may apply directly for the position of Lay Magistrate or apply following advertisements in the press for the position. The application is made to the Local Advisory Committee (LAC) which is made up of existing magistrates and other local people. An application form must be completed and references will be taken up.

The candidate will have to undergo two interviews:

Interview one

The LAC will check the candidate has the minimum eligibility requirements and look to see that they have the six key qualities. There will also be general questions asked to assess the candidate's attitude to various criminal justice issues such as, for example, drink driving.

Interview two

This interview is practically based and involves testing the candidate's potential judicial aptitude. The candidate will be given scenarios and asked to rank them in order of severity and will also be given a more in-depth case study based on sentencing practice.

If the candidate successfully completes both interviews and is deemed suitable, the LAC will submit the names to the Lord Chief Justice for approval before being submitted to the Lord Chancellor to make the appointment. The new magistrates are sworn in at an official ceremony, giving an oath of allegiance to the Queen.

Check your understanding

1. Identify the three formal requirements a person must fulfil in order to apply to become a lay magistrate.
2. Explain why a serving police officer is disqualified from sitting on the bench.
3. Explain why a person with a number of minor offences is disqualified from sitting on the bench.
4. Explain what is meant by the quality 'good character'.
5. Explain what is meant by the quality 'social awareness'.
6. What are the LAC looking for at the second interview?
7. Who appoints new lay magistrates on behalf of the Queen?

Answers on p.138

Training

Revised

The training of new magistrates is supervised by the Judicial College (formerly the Judicial Studies Board). The Court Act 2003 places a statutory obligation on the Lord Chancellor to provide training and training materials.

The Magistrates' New Training Initiative (MNTI 2) provides a competence framework which is divided into four areas of competency as follows:

● Managing yourself
● Working as a team member
● Making judicial decisions
● Managing judicial decisions (this competency is for Chairmen of the Bench).

First year training

In the first year, a trainee magistrate must complete:

1 **Initial training** – before sitting in court, the new magistrate is given introductory training on the basics of the role. They can then sit in court with experienced magistrates.

2 **Mentoring** – six formal mentored sittings in the first 12–18 months.

3 **Core training** – where the new magistrate must visit penal institutions and/or undertake court observations.

4 **Consolidation training**. This is at the end of the first year to build on the learning from the above and to prepare them for their first appraisal.

5 **First appraisal** – this takes place about 12–18 months after appointment and the mentor and magistrate agree he/she is ready and successfully deemed fully competent.

Extra training will be provided for those unable to demonstrate they have achieved the competencies. If they continue not to achieve these competencies, then the LAC will recommend to the Lord Chancellor that the magistrate is removed from sitting.

Retirement and removal

Magistrates retire at 70 years old; however, their names are added to the Supplementary List which means they can no longer sit in the Court but they can continue with some administrative duties. Under s 11 Courts Act 2003, the Lord Chancellor has the power to remove a lay magistrate for incapacity, persistent failure to meet competency standards or if they are deemed to be neglecting their duties. A magistrate can also be removed for misbehaviour.

Work/role   Revised

Criminal jurisdiction

● Magistrates' courts try 97% of all criminal cases from start to finish.

● They deal with the other 3% of criminal cases at least at a preliminary level with early administrative hearings (remand hearings, bail applications and committal proceedings).

● They deal with all summary matters – finding defendants not guilty or guilty and sentencing.

● In terms of triable-either-way matters, the lay magistrates will first undertake the 'plea before venue' procedure. If the defendant pleads guilty, then the lay magistrates will go ahead and sentence the defendant or pass the matter to the Crown Court for sentencing. If the defendant pleads not guilty, the lay magistrates will undertake a

Exam practice answers and quick quizzes at **www.therevisionbutton.co.uk/myrevisionnotes**

'mode of trial' hearing. During this they will decide whether or not they have sufficient jurisdiction to deal with the matter. If they decline jurisdiction, they will send the case for trial at the Crown Court.

- They deal with arrest and search warrants and extensions to detention time.
- Sit with judge in the Crown Court to hear appeals from the Magistrates' Court.
- Specially trained panels of magistrates deal with young offenders aged 10–17 years in Youth Courts.

Civil jurisdiction

- Specially trained panels of magistrates sit in the Family Court to hear cases including orders for protection against violence, affiliation cases, adoption orders and proceedings under the Children Act 1989.
- Enforce debts owed to the utilities, for example, electricity, gas and water.
- Deal with non-payment of Council Tax and TV licences.
- Hear appeals against the refusal of the Local Authority to grant a licence for the sale of alcohol and licences for betting and gaming establishments.

> **Typical mistake**
>
> Candidates miss out on valuable marks by omitting the civil jurisdiction of lay magistrates.

Who else sits in a Magistrates' Court?

District judges (Magistrates' Courts)

District judges (Magistrates' Courts) are members of the judiciary who hear cases in magistrates' courts. They are usually appointed to courts in big cities and deal with the more complex matters coming before the magistrates' courts. The District Judge will have been a qualified barrister or solicitor for at least five years or a Fellow of ILEX.

The Magistrates' Clerk

As the magistrates are not legally qualified, the bench is assisted by a clerk who will act as a legal advisor to the court. The clerk will have been a qualified barrister or solicitor for at least five years. The clerk's duty is to guide the magistrates on questions of law, practice and procedure.

Evaluation, including advantages and disadvantages

Revised ☐

There are many advantages and disadvantages of using lay magistrates in the English legal system. It is necessary for a student to be able to analyse central issues and develop clear arguments for and against their use. Set out in the table below are the key advantages and disadvantages.

Advantages	Disadvantages
Cost – cheaper than professional judges as unpaid (lay magistrates can only claim expenses and if they suffer loss of earnings, they may claim a loss allowance at a set rate).	Prosecution bias – lay magistrates have a tendency to side with the police and prosecution and as a result, the overall acquittal rate is considerably lower than that of the Crown Court.
Cross-section of society – wider than the judiciary. Campaign to attract a wider cross-section.	Reliance on the clerk – some magistrates rely too heavily on the clerk for advice.
Local knowledge – seen as an advantage as they will know the area well, including local crime 'hot spots'.	Inconsistency in sentencing – it has been said that it is a lottery as to what sentence you will receive. Some benches are more inclined to give custodial sentences, while another bench, for the same offence, is more likely to give community penalties.
Few appeals – there are comparatively few appeals from the Magistrates' Court, which indicates few errors of law and that they do a good job.	Middle-aged and middle class – a high percentage of lay magistrates are over the age of 40 and come from a managerial background. As a result, the bench is not a true cross-section of society.

Now test yourself

Tested ☐

See if you can answer the following question using the above P, D, W formula above. Use the table below.

1 Discuss the advantages and disadvantage of using lay magistrates to deal with criminal cases. **[12 marks]**

Point	Developed	Well developed
An advantage of using lay magistrates in criminal cases is that the magistrates come from the local area and therefore have local knowledge.		
An advantage of using lay magistrates is that they provide a cross-section of society in terms of gender, ethnic origin, age and social background.		
A disadvantage of using lay magistrates is that they lack any formal legal qualifications.		
A disadvantage of lay magistrates is that there is potential for bias as they get to know some of the prosecutors and police officers.		

Answers on p.139

Exam practice

a) Describe **both** the selection and the training of lay magistrates. **[18 marks]**

b) Discuss the **disadvantages** of using lay magistrates to deal with criminal cases. **[12 marks]**

OCR G151 June 2009

Answers and quick quizzes online

Online ☐

Exam practice answers and quick quizzes at **www.therevisionbutton.co.uk/myrevisionnotes**

Juries

Revised

This topic can be broken down into four distinct areas:

- qualifications, disqualifications, ineligibility and excusals
- selection, including vetting and challenging
- role
- evaluation, including advantages and disadvantages.

Two main skills are needed:

- Ability to describe, in detail, each of the above elements.
- Ability to analyse central issues and develop clear arguments.

Qualifications, disqualifications, inteligibility and excusals

Revised

Qualifications

The basic qualifications are set out in the Juries Act 1974 (as amended) as follows:

- aged between 18 and 70
- registered as a parliamentary or local government elector
- resident in UK for five years since age of 13.

Jurors must sit unless disqualified or excused.

Disqualifications

A person will be disqualified for life from serving on a jury if they have received the following sentences:

- imprisonment or detention for life
- detention during Her Majesty's Pleasure
- a term of imprisonment or detention of five years or more.

A person will be disqualified from serving on a jury for ten years if they have received the following sentences in the last ten years:

- a custodial sentence of less than 5 years
- a suspended sentence
- had a community order or other community sentence passed on them.

A person will also be disqualified whilst on bail.

Attending jury service and failing to declare any of the above will result in a fine of up to £5,000.

Ineligibility

- A person suffering from a 'mental disorder', as defined in the Criminal Justice Act 2003, cannot sit.
- Lacking capacity, for example, cannot speak English or suffering from a disability which results in the juror not being capable of acting effectively as a juror.

> **Exam tip**
>
> In order to obtain maximum marks for this part, it is necessary to do more than simply state that a person can be disqualified for being in prison. You need to add the detail as to how long and why a person might be disqualified.

Excusals

A person selected for jury service may ask to be excused. The following people may be excused:

- Full-time Armed Forces personnel if their commanding officer certifies that they are required for duty.
- A person with 'good reason' can be excused or have service deferred. This is at the discretion of the court and reasons for this may be, for example, examinations, business commitments and illness.

Simply ignoring the summons and not attending court may result in a fine of up to £1,000.

Lawyers, judges and police officers on juries

The Criminal Justice Act 2003 changed who was and who was not eligible for jury service. The Act abolished the rule that people involved in the administration of justice were ineligible to serve on a jury. This included lawyers, judges and police officers.

Check your understanding

8 Identify the basic qualifications required to sit on the jury.

9 Name two sentences which will disqualify a person for life from serving on a jury.

10 How long will a person be disqualified from serving on a jury if they have previously received a suspended sentence?

11 Identify why a person may be ineligible to serve due to lack of capacity.

12 When will a full-time member of the Armed Forces be excused from jury duty?

13 Which Act of Parliament changed the eligibility rules and allowed judges to serve on a jury?

Answers on p.138

Selection, including vetting and challenging   Revised ☐

Selection

- A Crown Court official will, at random from the electoral registers, summons enough jurors to try cases every fortnight. In the larger courts up to 150 summonses are sent out at one time.
- Summonses are sent out electronically using a computer at central office, notifying a person of when and where they are to attend.
- At court in the first instance, 15 potential jurors are chosen at random from the jury pool to go into the court room.
- Twelve are then chosen at random in court by the clerk.

Jurors are shown a short film when they arrive in court which explains to them the procedure in court and how to behave, including not discussing the case with any other person.

Vetting

Both the prosecution and defence have the right to see the list of potential jurors and may decide that the pool needs to be 'vetted'. There are two types of vetting:

- Routine police checks to eliminate those disqualified as approved in *R v Mason* (1980).
- Wider background check for political affiliations; however, this is rarely used and the Attorney-General's guidelines must be adhered to.

Challenging

Once the 12 jurors have been selected but before they are sworn in, both the prosecution and defence have the right to challenge one or more of the jury. There are three types of challenges; the first two are available to both the defence and the prosecution. The final one is only available to the prosecution.

1 Challenge to the array on way jury selected, for example, chosen in an unrepresentative or bias way. Used successfully against the 'Romford' jury where two of the jurors lived in the same street. However, the challenge will not be allowed simply because the jury is not multi-racial – *R v Ford* (1989).

2 Challenge for cause – challenging a person's right to be on the jury because of connection with the case (*R v Wilson* (1996) and *R v Sprason* (1995)) or incapacity.

3 Right of stand-by jurors (only available to the prosecution) allows a member of the jury to be put at the end of the list so that they will not be used unless there are not enough jurors.

AO2 assessment – criticisms of selection

- Electoral register does not include all the population as it excludes homeless people.
- No power to ensure multi-racial juries.
- Some disqualified jurors may sit and those given certain sentences are still eligible.
- Excusals were too many at one stage – now more difficult to get an excusal and this may lead to resentment.

> **Typical mistake**
>
> Omitting vetting and challenging when answering a question on selection.

Role

Role in criminal trials

The role in criminal matters is split between the judge and the jury. The judge presides over the case and decides points of law. The jury's role is to decide the facts. If the judge decides that, in law, the prosecution's evidence has not made out a case against the defendant, s/he will direct the jury to acquit. The judge will pass the sentence at the end of the case.

- A jury is only used in a small percentage of criminal cases.
- They sit in the Crown Court and decide whether the defendant is guilty or not guilty in serious cases.
- They listen to the evidence from both the prosecution and the defence and, at the end of the trial, listen to the summing up by the judge.
- They decide questions of fact; the judge will advise them on questions of law.
- At the end of the trial they retire to the jury room to discuss the case in secret and, if possible, come to a unanimous decision or, if directed by the judge, a majority decision of at least 10–2, if necessary.
- They do not have to give any reasons for their decisions.
- The judge must accept the verdict of the jury.

Role in civil cases

Juries are rarely used in civil cases but can be used in both the County and the High Court. They are mainly used in defamation cases. In the High Court, the jury will be made up of 12 members and in the County Court there will be eight members. In civil matters the jury has a dual role as they decide both the verdict and assess damages to be awarded.

Typical mistake

Candidates miss out on valuable marks by omitting the civil role played by jurors.

- Jury trial is only available only in four types of case in the High Court or County Court:
  - defamation
  - false imprisonment
  - malicious prosecution
  - fraud.
- Only retained for these cases because they deal with character or reputation.
- A judge can refuse to allow a jury in these cases if they think the evidence is too complicated.
- In exceptional circumstances a personal injury case in the High Court can use a jury. But since the case of *Ward v James* (1966) no personal injury case has been deemed exceptional.

Using juries in Civil Courts AO2 assessment issues

There are particular problems of using juries in civil trials, for example:

- Civil juries decide both the verdict and the amount of damages. In terms of damages, juries do not use past precedent and therefore it is extremely difficult to predict the amount of damages that will be awarded, which causes difficulty for lawyers advising clients.
- If public figures are involved there may be bias.
- Cost of using a jury makes the case much more expensive for the losing party.

Coroner's Court

Juries are used in the Coroner's Court to enquire into suspicious deaths, for example, when death occurred while in custody or the cause of death is unknown. There will be between seven and eleven jurors used.

Evaluation, including advantages and disadvantages of using juries

Revised

There are many advantages and disadvantages of using juries in the English legal system. It is necessary for a student to be able to analyse central issues and develop clear arguments for and against their use. Set out in the table below are the key advantages and disadvantages.

Advantages	Disadvantages
Public confidence – one of the fundamentals of a democratic society. As Lord Devlin said, juries are 'The lamp that shows that freedom lives'.	Perverse decisions – can be a protest against the law, but is it up to a jury?
Jury equity – decide on fairness not just the law (*Kronlid* (1996), *Ponting* (1985))	Jury tampering by, for example, bribery or threats. This may lead to trial by judge alone – *R v Twomey and others* (2009).
Open system of justice – justice is seen to be done.	Racial bias as there is no right to a multi-racial jury – *Saunder v UK* (2000).
Lawyers have to explain matters simply (no technical jargon) thus allowing D and the public to follow proceedings.	Media coverage may influence jurors – *R v West* (1996), *R v Taylor and Taylor* (1993).
Allows the ordinary person to take part in the administration of justice.	Lack of understanding – especially for fraud trials, which are extremely complex and the trial can last a very long time.
Secrecy of the jury room – allows the jury to be free of outside pressure.	Secrecy of the jury room – it is unknown how they make the decision and there may be questionable decisions which cannot be appealed – *R v Mirza* and *R v Connor and Rollock* (2004). However, this does not include suspicious practice outside the jury room – *R v Young (Stephen)* (1995).

When assessing juries, it is worth looking at the alternatives on offer and considering the pros and cons of these, for example:

- trial by a single judge
- a panel of judges
- a judge plus lay assessors
- a mini jury.

Typical mistake

- Getting juries muddled up with magistrates.
- Not answering the question – especially on part (b) questions, giving both advantages and disadvantages when only one was required.
- Lack of detail.

Exam tip

A part (b) 'discuss' question may ask you to discuss the advantages and/or the disadvantages of juries in general. However, it may ask you to discuss a more specific issue, for example, whether or not juries should be retained (kept) (see OCR, G151, Jan 2009 Question 4(b)) or the advantages and/or disadvantages of the secrecy of the jury room (see OCR, G151, June 2010 Question 5(b)).

Now test yourself

Tested ☐

2 Compare the role of juries in civil and criminal cases.

	In criminal cases	In civil cases
When used?		
What do they do?		
What do they decide?		
Unanimous?		
Where does discussion take place?		

Answers on p.139

Exam practice

a) Describe the qualifications and selection procedure for choosing a jury. **[18 marks]**

b) Discuss the arguments for and against keeping the secrecy of the jury room. **[12 marks]**

OCR, G151, June 2010

Answers and quick quizzes online

Online ☐

8 Provision of legal services

What you need to know about the provision of legal services:

Government funding, which covers:

- criminal legal advice and representation
- legal advice availability
- access to justice
- civil legal funding.

Private funding, which covers:

- private work by lawyers
- conditional fee arrangements
- some advice agencies.

Three main skills are needed to answer a legal services question:

- An ability to describe in detail the law relating to each area for part a) of questions in both sections of the paper.
- Development of analytical and critical points for Section A part b) discussion questions.
- Application of relevant law for Section B part b) scenario questions.

Government funding

Revised ☐

Government funding is the subject of many reform proposals with availability being reduced and contributions being increased in general. At the moment it is overseen by the Legal Services Commission which was set up by the Access to Justice Act 1999.

Funding for criminal cases

The Access to Justice Act 1999 established the Criminal Defence Service which offers:

- duty solicitor schemes
- advice and assistance at the Magistrates' Court
- representation.

The duty solicitor scheme at the police station

- Run by local contracted solicitors with relevant qualification ('Police Station Qualification').
- Available to anyone questioned at the police station but will only be by telephone unless attendance will 'materially progress the case'.
- Covers advice and attending interviews but attendance is limited unless the client is vulnerable.
- Free to all, no means or merits testing.

Advice and assistance

- Franchised solicitor.
- Covers advice and some preparatory work for someone charged with an offence and help with their application for legal representation, limited to one hour's work.

Exam practice answers and quick quizzes at **www.therevisionbutton.co.uk/myrevisionnotes**

- Means tested – only those on very low incomes qualify.
- If at the Magistrates' Court – contracted solicitor with relevant qualification (Magistrates' Court Qualification) acts under the duty solicitor scheme, whereas it is free for anyone in custody.

Legal representation

- Franchised solicitor or independent barrister.
- Covers representation and all steps in preparation of a case.
- Merits tested (interests of justice).
- Means test in the Magistrates' Court – difficult to qualify unless on benefits or under 18 years old.
- Means test in the Crown Court where contributions depend on both income and type of case, may have to pay extra from capital if found guilty.
- If found not guilty, contributions will be returned.

Discussion points on criminal legal funding

- Budget has not been increased with inflation which has led to cuts in availability.
- Means testing for criminal legal funding for representation in the Magistrates' Court has been re-introduced and only 25% of adults are eligible.
- Trials in the Magistrates' Court are less expensive than in the Crown Court but a lack of funding can cause real hardship to families.
- It will still tend to be free for repeat offenders as they are less likely to be employed.
- The merits test – in the interests of justice, this is now applied very strictly, which leads to repeat offenders having representation but first-time offenders not getting representation as they are less likely to be imprisoned. This cannot be seen as fair.
- Means testing for Crown Court cases has been brought in which could seriously disadvantage some defendants as they are much more expensive to fund, depending on the type of case (although if they are found not guilty their payments are refunded).
- Few lawyers are willing to work for the fixed fees offered by the government so it is difficult for defendants to find a local solicitor to take their case anyway.

Now test yourself

Tested

1 Complete the following table.

Type of help	What it covers	Means or merits test?
Duty Solicitor Scheme		
Advice and assistance in criminal cases		
Representation in criminal cases		

Answers on p.140

Now test yourself

2 Try to identify the issues in the following scenario and conclude whether the funding criteria have been applied correctly to Thomas.

Thomas (aged 30) has been arrested on suspicion of manslaughter. He is unemployed and has a limited grasp of the English language but is only offered advice from a solicitor over the phone. He is charged and a duty solicitor at the Magistrates' Court gives him some advice regarding his bail application. He is told he cannot be funded in the Crown Court as it is not in the interests of justice and he will have to pay if he wants representation.

Answers on p.140

Civil funding

You will need to know how the Community Legal Service works under the Access to Justice Act 1999:

- How the Community Legal fund is funded by the Legal Services Commission.
- What is excluded from funding and the priorities for funding.
- The effect of a finite fund.
- The different types of help available, from advice to representation.
- Means testing – funding criteria and contributions.
- Merits testing.

Overseen by the Legal Services Commission but moving to the Ministry of Justice and administered by the Community Legal Service and covers:

- legal help, which is confined to advice
- help at court advice and help short of representation
- legal representation at court
- support funding which is partial funding for a case.

There is a budget allocated for civil funding which tends to run out every year so even if a person falls within all the criteria they may not get funding.

Criteria for funding legal representation in civil cases:

- Means tested on disposable capital and disposable income. The limits are quite low, allowing those on income-based befits to qualify and very few others.
- Merits test based on likelihood of success and amount of damages likely to be awarded and the conduct of the parties.
- Priorities for funding as there is a finite fund.
- Some matters excluded, e.g. personal injury, wills, boundary disputes, defamation and more recently divorce.
- Not available for cases involving less than £5,000.
- Not available for tribunals except mental health.

Discussion points on how access to public funding affects access to justice:

- Finite fund – where there is a limited budget, it has to be rationed.
- Eligibility levels for legal funding are very low so that only the poorest have access to justice, those of even a moderate income or homeowners do not have such access.

Exam practice answers and quick quizzes at **www.therevisionbutton.co.uk/myrevisionnotes**

- There are not enough providers of publicly funded services in certain parts of the country, leading to advice deserts. This limits access to those who can travel or live in the right area.
- Funding is becoming less available with fewer types of case being eligible. With some types of case, there is the alternative of a conditional fee agreement such as personal injury but it is very difficult to get for a divorce unless there is domestic violence and there is no real alternative available for anyone with few assets.

Now test yourself

Tested ☐

3 Complete the following table.

Type of help	What it covers	Means or merits test?
Civil legal help		
Help at court for a civil case		
Legal representation in civil cases		

Answers on p.140

Advice agencies

Available from a wide range of providers but there are areas where advice is limited to internet or telephone unless a person is willing to travel considerable distances.

- The Legal Services Commission grants contracts to firms of solicitors
- The Community Legal Service website
- Citizens Advice Bureaux
- Law Centres
- Charities, e.g. Shelter
- Motoring organisations
- Consumer organisations, e.g. *Which*
- Legal insurance
- National telephone helpline
- Internet advice.

Private funding

Solicitors offer representation and advice to anyone who can pay for it but much work is done under the conditional fee option.

Conditional fees

For a Section A question, you need to be able to explain:

- what a conditional fee agreement is
- the fact that it is the only way to fund personal injury cases now if funding is required
- how they work.

For Section B questions, you need to be able to discuss:

- what problems can occur such as paying for insurance premiums
- whether they can be regarded as successfully providing more access to justice.

Conditional fees were developed to help people deal with the risk of taking a case to court as costs are uncertain and there is always a risk of losing the case.

- Solicitor and client agree on a fee which would normally be charged for a particular case.
- Success fee is agreed up to 100% of normal fee added to fee if case is won but cannot exceed 25% of damages.
- If case is lost, solicitor gets nothing.
- Success fee may be ordered to be paid by losing party.
- Insurance is taken out to protect against paying costs of other side if case is lost. This premium can also be claimed from the losing party.

Discussion points on how conditional fees affect access to justice:

- Many areas of civil law are removed from legal funding and have to rely on conditional fee agreements which have many problems.
- Some large firms dealing with conditional fee agreements have gone into liquidation, showing the difficulty of making a profit unless cases are carefully screened before taking them on.
- Levels of compensation agreed by large firms thought to be lower than those negotiated by independent solicitors.
- Difficult to find solicitors to deal with risky cases.
- Difficult for lawyers to estimate costs in complicated cases so some cases make a loss, even with 100% uplift fee.
- Clients may feel obliged to settle early at a lower level of compensation.

Typical mistake

- Lack of detail. This topic is often answered badly purely due to lack of revision.
- Not really answering the question.
- 'This is all I know about public funding' answers, regardless of the question.
- Confusing public funding with private funding.
- Confusing advice with representation.
- Only answering half the question.
- Answering a different question to the one asked.

Exam summary

How do we avoid these common mistakes?

- ✔ Read the question carefully.
- ✔ Ensure you are clear on the difference between public funding and private funding.
- ✔ Ensure you put in some detail (do not make lists without detail).
- ✔ If the question is about criminal funding, remember to cover both advice and representation.
- ✔ Do not waste time on discussing the merits of legal funding or its problems as this is not required in Section A questions and gets no marks.

Exam practice answers and quick quizzes at **www.therevisionbutton.co.uk/myrevisionnotes**

How to answer a Section A question

- If the question asks for a description of civil legal funding, try to cover all the main points – the Community Legal Service Fund, types of help, what is excluded and the means and merits tests.
- If the question asks for a description of Criminal Legal Funding, ensure you cover the duty solicitor schemes, advice and assistance and representation including the Public Defender Service.
- Stick to the question.
- Put in as much detail as possible.
- Remember to use statutory authority. Describe the qualifications, selection and training of judges.

How to answer a Section A question on criminal legal funding

Describe the different publicly funded advice and representation available to a person suspected of and then charged with an offence.

First **plan** your answer.

This sort of question needs a commonsense approach as you need to work out a logical sequence to deal with several types of publicly funded advice and representation.

Start with the first that would be used and then progress though the system step by step. You are only giving information – you do not need to comment in Section A questions.

- Publicly funded advice and representation for criminal cases is provided by the Criminal Defence Service who are responsible for several schemes.
- The Duty Solicitor scheme at the police station is run by local contracted solicitors with a Police Station qualification. It is available to anyone questioned at the police station but may only be permitted by telephone in many cases unless the solicitor can show that attendance was necessary to 'materially progress the case'. It covers advice and attending interviews and is free to all, regardless of their income – there is no means or merits testing.
- From the police station a person charged with an offence would move on to the Magistrate's Court. The Duty Solicitor scheme at the Magistrates' Court allows free access to a solicitor for defendants in custody, but only very limited access for one hour of a solicitor's time, and that is strictly means tested by the solicitor.
- A contracted solicitor with a relevant qualification (Magistrates' Court qualification) would be used and can give advice and help with their application for representation.

Finally you would need to describe when legal representation would be available.
- The Legal Representation scheme covers representation and all steps in the preparation of a case.
- It is provided by a franchised solicitor or independent barrister but it is merits tested (interests of justice) and means tested in both the Magistrates' Court and more recently the Crown Court. It is difficult to qualify unless on benefits or under 18 years old. A convicted defendant may be ordered to pay costs at the end of the case.

That illustrates the simplicity of Section A questions.

All you need to do is learn the material, select the correct parts for the question and write as many details as you can remember in a logical sequence.

How to answer a question on civil funding and conditional fees

Describe how civil cases are funded by the Community Legal Service and by conditional fee agreements.
As you only have 20 minutes to answer this question you need to be very concise.
There are **two fairly equal parts** to the question so you should spend **ten minutes** on each part.

- Firstly you should explain that the Community Legal Fund is used to fund eligible civil cases; however, it is a limited fund and there are priorities for funding such as domestic violence cases.
- Some matters are excluded as a matter of priority, e.g. personal injury, wills, boundary disputes and defamation cases.

- It is also not available for cases involving less than £5,000 or for tribunals, except mental health.
- It is means tested on both disposable capital and disposable income.
- You should then go on to describe conditional fee agreements by explaining that they were developed to help people to deal with the risk of taking a case to court as costs are uncertain, and often very high, and there is always a risk of losing the case.
- The solicitor and client agree on a fee that would normally be charged for a particular case. A success fee is agreed, with up to 100% of the normal fee added to the fee if the case is won but the success fee cannot exceed 25% of damages. If the case is lost, solicitor gets nothing,
- The success fee may be ordered to be paid by the losing party. Insurance is taken out to protect against paying the costs of the other side if the case is lost. This premium can also be claimed off the losing party.

This is a very concise answer and more detail would really be needed for the best marks.

Typical mistake

- The most common mistake with any discussion question is a failure to actually discuss anything and to just give information.
- It is also common to see answers where the candidate has made some attempt to discuss in a limited way by saying something is good or bad but without giving a reason.
- There is sometimes confusion about the subject matter of the question.
- Lack of knowledge of the subject is as fatal to the production of a good Section B answer as it is to a good Section A answer.
- Lack of evidence to back up any arguments.
- Lack of any conclusion to the answer.

Exam summary

What sort of discussion questions could be asked?

✔ The question could relate to the need for state funding of cases for those who cannot afford to pay for it themselves.

✔ You could be asked to discuss whether the present system of criminal legal funding is satisfactory or in need of reform.

✔ You could be asked a similar question on civil legal funding, or conditional fees.

✔ You could be asked to consider whether the availability of legal advice is adequate to meet the needs of the people.

Exam summary

The best way to produce a good Section B answer to a discussion question

✔ Answer the question in a logical sequence and deal with the issues one at a time.

✔ Set out each fact and then comment on it.

✔ Clearly link your answer back to the question asked.

✔ Try to produce a balanced argument.

✔ Ensure you are able to quote some statistics and have thought out arguments for all possible questions.

✔ Write a concluding paragraph.

G152 Sources of Law

Key skills in G152

Success in G152 will require **three** key skills:

1 Knowledge of the relevant area of law in parts a) and c (i) with precise definitions, clear explanations and appropriate use of supporting examples such as cases, statutes or other illustrations.

2 The ability to apply legal knowledge and principles to problem questions in part b) whilst successfully identifying the critical issue in the question.

3 Evaluative, critical and analytical skills in part c (ii) which facilitate discussion of the relevant area of law in some wider context such as effectiveness, advantages and disadvantages or broader impact.

Number 1 counts as assessment objective 1 (AO1) and numbers 2 and 3 count as assessment objective 2 (AO2). For more information, assessment materials, past papers, mark schemes and the specification, please refer to **http://www.ocr.org.uk/qualifications/as-a-level-gce-law-h134-h534/**

Important constitutional principles in sources of law   `Revised` ☐

G152 'Sources of Law' is, essentially, all about where our main laws come from, how they are applied and interpreted and their wider effect. It will be helpful to understand a few key legal doctrines that are particularly relevant to sources of law.

Parliamentary sovereignty

The doctrine of parliamentary sovereignty (or 'supremacy') holds that Parliament is the supreme law-making authority. Parliament is made up of the House of Commons, the House of Lords and the Monarch and laws made by Parliament cannot be overruled, altered or set aside except by a later Act of Parliament.

Separation of powers

This doctrine is attributed to a French political theorist called Charles Montesquieu. Montesquieu put forward the idea that a state could be identified as having three parts: an executive who propose new laws and administer the state, a legislature who pass the laws and a judiciary who apply and interpret the laws. Montesquieu believed that these three functions must remain separate because if an individual or body were able to exercise power in more than one function, this might lead to abuse of power.

Judicial independence

The independence of the judiciary is one of the cornerstones of the English legal system. Judges have to make decisions which can have a profound effect on the lives of individuals, businesses and even the state itself. It is essential, therefore, that judges are able to operate without any kind of political, financial or other influence. A number of protections exist (see G151) to ensure the independence of the judiciary and this, in turn, allows the judiciary to take controversial decisions without fear of censure.

The rule of law

The rule of law can mean different things in different contexts but within G152, the meaning is that we distinguish the rule of law from the rule of men. The rule of men might embrace monarchies that abuse their power or dictatorships who make unfair and unjust rules. The rule of law, on the other hand, says that individuals, businesses and even government itself will submit to, obey and be regulated by the ordinary law of the land in the ordinary courts and not to arbitrary action by an individual or a group of individuals. Put simply, everyone is equal before the ordinary law of the land.

1 Doctrine of precedent

Revised ☐

What is it?

Precedent is the process by which judges follow the decisions of previous judges where the facts of the case before them are sufficiently similar to the facts of the earlier case.

Key terms

Precedent is the term used to refer to the body of law built up by judges over hundreds of years in the courts of common law. Confusingly, as well as precedent, it is sometimes also referred to as common law, judge-made law or case law but these are all the same thing.

It is based on the Latin saying *'stare decisis et non quieta movere'* which means (roughly) 'stand by what has been decided and do not unsettle the established'. We refer to it as simply *stare decisis* for short which means to stand by decided matters.

It is, arguably, our oldest and most important source of law and forms the basis of some of our most fundamental areas of law.

Why do we have it?

Revised ☐

Rules in general should be fair, just, objective, consistent and rational. If they are not, people will not respect them or obey them. The same is true of legal rules. Like cases should be treated alike. This allows people to plan their actions in full knowledge of the possible consequences and it allows lawyers to accurately predict the likely outcome of a particular case. Thus, precedent provides certainty, predictability and stability to the legal system.

How does it operate?

Revised ☐

In order to operate properly, precedent needs:

- a system of case reporting because there are too many laws to be passed on by word of mouth so they must be accurately recorded somewhere so that future judges can refer back to them. Recording all the important judgments is known as law reporting.

- a clear hierarchy of courts so that each court or judge knows who he or she should follow

- a method of identifying the parts of a judgment which bind a judge from the other parts which need not be followed and can be overruled.

Mechanics of precedent

Precedent as operated in the English legal system

The way that the rules of precedent operate through the doctrine of *stare decisis* can be referred to as the 'mechanics of precedent'. The skills required in this section will be the ability to:

- describe the mechanics of precedent including the exceptions to the general rules;
- apply your knowledge of the rules of precedent to a given scenario;
- discuss the way that precedent affects the legal system and the way that judges operate the system.

Law reporting

If courts are to follow previous decisions then they need to refer to some accurate record of those earlier decisions. These are known as law reports. Law reports have existed since at least the 13th century but until 1865 they were variable in quality and reliability. In 1865 the Incorporated Council of Law Reporting was set up under the authority of the court system. These reports are considered more accurate and reliable and remain one of the principal sources of decisions of the superior and appellate courts.

There are a number of other well-established reports which follow an approved format, the most significant of which being the All England series which reports many major cases from 1936 onwards (including a so-called reprint of leading cases from 1558 to 1936).

Nowadays, many of these reports are made available in the form of commercial searchable databases such as LexisNexis and Westlaw and free online resources such as the Supreme Court website and BAILII (British and Irish Legal Information).

The parts of a judgment – *obiter dicta* and *ratio decidendi*

A judgment is written in continuous prose and will usually contain a review of the facts of the case, some consideration of the evidence offered, some broad legal reasoning, a review of relevant legal authorities (case law and statute), the specific legal reasoning applied in the particular case and the actual decision. Somewhere within this judgment will be the legal principle of the case. This is the legal rule and associated reasoning behind the decision and is known as the *ratio decidendi* (or *ratio* for short). Once the *ratio* is identified, everything else in a judgment is known as the *obiter dicta* which means 'said by the way' or 'said in passing'. It must be remembered that it is the legal reason behind the decision which is the *ratio* not the factual outcome of the case.

For example, in *R v Bentham* (2005) a man robbed his former employer. In order to do so, he held his hand inside a zipped up jacket with his fingers pointing so as to give the impression that he had a gun. He was convicted and on appeal the court had to decide whether he was guilty of possessing an imitation firearm. The court decided that he could not. The legal reasoning behind this decision can be seen about two-thirds of the way into Lord Bingham's judgment where he states *'one cannot possess something which is not separate and distinct from oneself'*. It is this reasoning which is the *ratio* of *R v Bentham* not the fact that Bentham won his appeal.

Key terms

Ratio – the legal principle of a case – not the factual outcome.
Obiter – the other parts of the judgment once the *ratio* has been identified.

The *ratio* of a case becomes the binding precedent (see below) of that case. However, the *obiter* may contain legal principles which are also followed by later cases. For example, in *Donoghue v Stevenson* (1932) a lady was ill after consuming the decomposing remains of a snail which were in the opaque bottle of ginger beer a friend had bought her. She could not sue the café as she had not purchased the ginger beer so she sued the manufacturer. At the time of the case there was no duty owed between a manufacturer of a product and the end consumer, due largely to the possibility of intermediate interference. However, Lord Atkin set out the *ratio* of the case thus:

> 'a manufacturer of products, which he sells in such a form as to show that he intends them to reach the ultimate consumer in the form in which they left him with no reasonable possibility of intermediate examination, and with the knowledge that the absence of reasonable care in the preparation or putting up of the products will result in an injury to the consumer's life or property, owes a duty to the consumer to take that reasonable care.'

However, the case has become more famous for something Lord Atkin said in his *obiter* comments. Lord Atkin was trying to set out a general rule or principle which could be used to establish the existence of a duty of care in negligence rather than sticking to a narrow range of existing duty situations. It has become known as the neighbour principle and has formed the basis of the modern law of negligence:

> '... acts or omissions which any moral code would censure cannot in a practical world be treated so as to give a right to every person injured by them to demand relief. In this way rules of law arise which limit the range of complaints and the extent of their remedy. The (moral) rule that you are to love your neighbour becomes in law, you must not injure your neighbour; and the lawyer's question, "Who is my neighbour?" receives a restricted reply. You must take reasonable care to avoid acts or omissions which you can reasonably foresee would be likely to injure your neighbour. Who, then, in law is my neighbour? The answer seems to be – persons who are so closely and directly affected by my act that I ought to have them in contemplation as being so affected when I am directing my mind to the acts or omissions which are called in question.'

Other well known examples of *obiter dicta* which have gone on to become important might include the comments of Lord Denning in *Central London Property Trust Ltd v High Trees House Ltd* (1947) where the doctrine of equitable estoppel was developed despite not having relevance to the case itself on its facts.

More than one judgment?

Many appeal cases are heard by a panel of judges. These are usually panels of three but may be five, seven or even larger in some exceptional circumstances. Ideally, the court will reach a unanimous decision but the requirement is only to reach a majority decision. A unanimous panel may all decide to follow the lead judgment as they did in *R v Bentham* (above), in which case a single judgment will be produced which the other judges agree with. Alternatively, all the judges will publish their own judgments. However, where there is a minority against, the minority judges still publish their judgments and these are known as 'dissenting judgments'.

Now test yourself

1 Research the case of *R v Howe* (1987) and find out what the *ratio* was. What was the *obiter* comment that was later followed in *R v Gotts* (1992)?

Answers on p.141

Tested

The hierarchy of the courts

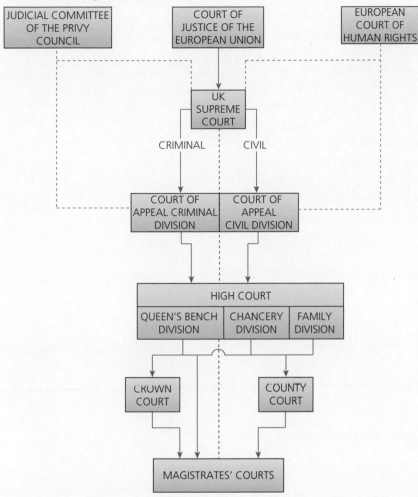

Figure 1.1 The hierarchy of the courts

The European Court of Human Rights

The European Court of Human Rights (ECtHR), which has nothing whatsoever to do with the EU, is the judicial arm of the European Convention on Human Rights. Before the Human Rights Act (1998) (HRA) was passed, the UK courts treated the decisions of the ECtHR as persuasive only. There was no duty on a UK court to follow an ECtHR decision although they frequently did so (*Malone v UK* (1984)). Since the passing of the HRA, the Convention has become part of domestic law. Section 2 of the HRA requires UK courts to 'take into account' any decision of the ECtHR in so far as they are relevant in cases concerning a Convention right. This means that domestic courts are required to take account of all the legal decisions of the ECtHR, not merely those cases brought against the UK, but are not bound by it.

The question of what a UK court should do when an earlier decision of a higher domestic court conflicts with a later ECtHR case was answered recently in *Kay and Others v Lambeth Borough Council* and *Leeds City Council v Price* (2006). Lord Bingham said that the ordinary rules of precedent must apply and the higher domestic court must be followed in the interests of certainty.

> ## Key terms
>
> The court '**hierarchy**' is another way of saying 'pecking order'. In the context of precedent it just means that courts higher up the pecking order (hierarchy) bind courts lower down.

The Judicial Committee of the Privy Council

The Judicial Committee of the Privy Council (JCPC) does not bind any English court. However, because the composition of the JCPC is almost entirely made up of Supreme Court Justices, its decisions (on points of law relevant to English law) are strongly persuasive. There have been unusual instances where domestic courts have chosen to follow the JCPC rather than an ordinarily binding domestic precedent. For example, in *Doughty v Turner Manufacturing* (1964) the Court of Appeal preferred the JCPC decision in *The Wagon Mound* (1961) to its own previous decision in *Re Polemis* (1921). More recently, in *R v James* (2006) the Court of Appeal preferred to follow the JCPC decision in *Attorney-General for Jersey v Holley* (2005) to the House of Lords decision in *R v Smith (Morgan)* (2004). The reason which seems to have been impliedly accepted by the House of Lords was that the composition of the JCPC consisted of half of the entire House of Lords, the judgment contained a definitive clarification of the English law at issue and the outcome of any appeal to the House of Lords would have been a foregone conclusion.

The Court of Justice of the European Union

The CJEU consists of three courts: the Court of Justice, the General Court and the Civil Service Tribunal.

UK courts are bound by the CJEU but only on matters of EU law (s 3 European Communities Act (1972)) as seen in *R v Secretary of State for Transport ex parte Factortame Ltd.*

The United Kingdom Supreme Court (UKSC) (formerly the House of Lords)

The UKSC binds all domestic courts, both civil and criminal. It is generally bound by its own previous decisions subject to the exception of using the Practice Statement (1966) (see below).

The Court of Appeal

The Court of Appeal is bound by the CJEU and the UKSC and it, in turn, binds all domestic courts below it. The Court of Appeal is bound by its own previous decisions subject to limited exceptions (see below), but the two divisions of the Court of Appeal do not bind each other.

The High Court

The High Court is bound by the CJEU, the UKSC and the Court of Appeal and it, in turn, binds all the inferior courts below it.

The Inferior Courts

The inferior courts are all bound by the courts above them. They do not generally produce precedent and do not generally bind each other.

Now test yourself

Tested

2 An appeal case involving breach of contract is decided by the Court of Appeal (Civil Division). Who will be bound by this decision? *High, counts, magistrates, divisional* *↗ typically mag*

all the other courts but not bound

3 A case involving the defence of insanity is heard in the Crown Court. Who will be bound by this decision?

4 An appeal involving the Human Rights Act has been determined by the ECtHR. Who will be bound by this decision?

5 An appeal involving employment rights under an EU Regulation has been determined by the CJEU. Who will be bound by this decision?

6 An appeal involving sentencing practice has been determined by the UKSC. Who will be bound by this decision?

Answers on p.141

Type of precedent	Meaning	Features	Example
Binding	A precedent which **must** be followed.	This usually operates through the court hierarchy because the binding precedent comes from an earlier case of a higher court. It may be binding because it is a previous decision of the present court and no exception applies. In order to be bound there will have to be similar material facts. The *obiter* of one case can develop into the ratio of another case – **R v Ahluwalia (1992)** (obiter) into **R v Dryden (1995)** (ratio). The binding precedent is found in the ratio of the case. Cases are capable of having more than one binding precedent – **Read v J Lyons & Co (1947)**.	**Donoghue v Stevenson (1932)** – that a manufacturer of a product is liable to the end consumer of that product.
Original	A precedent which involves a point of law that has **never been decided before**.	When a new decision is made it becomes both a new binding precedent (for the applicable courts) and a new original precedent. Original precedents can be a response to problems with existing laws or changing moral and social standards as well as wider economic and technological changes. Original precedents can form the basis of the development of new legal principles – in **Donoghue v Stevenson (1932)**, the principles were followed in **Grant v Australian Knitting Mills (1936)**. One of the techniques used by judges when arriving at original precedents is known as 'reasoning by analogy'. This happens where a judge relies on a similar broad principle in an earlier case and compares it to the present novel case to produce an original precedent – **Hunter v Canary Wharf (1995)** (loss of TV reception) reasoned by analogy with **Aldred's Case (1611)** (loss of a view). Judges who issue original precedents can be accused of judicial law-making but they would argue in their defence that they are simply applying known legal principles to a novel situation (so-called Declaratory Theory) – **Airedale NHS Trust v Bland (1993)**.	**Re S (adult: refusal of medical treatment) (1992)** – medical treatment (a Caesarean section) against the mother's wishes was lawful based on the best interests of the child.
Persuasive	This is a precedent in which the judge can look at the legal principles in other cases and if he/she is 'persuaded' by the legal reasoning then he/she may decide to follow that case and is said to have been **persuaded** by it.	There are a number of sources of persuasive precedents: Courts lower in the hierarchy: The judgment from a lower court may persuade a higher court. This is especially so between the Court of Appeal and the United Kingdom Supreme Court (House of Lords). Decisions of the Judicial Committee of the Privy Council: Due to the fact that this court is composed of many of our most senior judges, some of their decisions are considered highly persuasive despite the fact that the court has no binding authority on domestic courts. Statements made *obiter dicta*: *Obiter dicta* statements can be persuasive especially when they contain the thinking of the most senior courts and judges. A dissenting judgement: Where a judge on a panel of judges disagrees with the majority, he/she will give his/her reasons. It is possible that on appeal to a higher court, that they may be persuaded by the reasoning in the dissenting judgment. Decisions of courts in other countries: Especially where that country uses the same principles of common law as our own as in, for instance, countries of the former Empire like Australia, New Zealand and Canada.	For example, in **R v R (1991)** the House of Lords agreed with the Court of Appeal in ruling that a man could be guilty of raping his wife. A well-known example is **The Wagon Mound (No.1) (1961)** regarding remoteness of damage in negligence. A well-known example has already been referred to above **(R v Howe (1987)** and **R v Gotts (1992))** regarding the availability of the defence of duress. An example being **Rose & Frank Co v JR Crompton & Bros Ltd (1924)** regarding the enforceability of contracts. **R v Bentham (2005)** (above) considered a number of American authorities as the case involved possession of a gun (which is lawful in many parts of the USA).

Fill in the gaps below.

7   The UKSC has been dealing with a case on insanity. A similar case from Hong Kong was decided by the Privy Council 20 years ago. The UKSC can *choose* whether to follow the Hong Kong case as it is only *persuasive*.

8   The Court of Appeal is dealing with an unusual case concerning stealing money by hacking into a computer and transferring funds to a foreign bank account. There is no English authority on the point of law so the Court of Appeal makes an *original* precedent which future *lower* courts will now have to follow.

9   The Crown Court must follow the decision of the Court of Appeal as it is *binding* This is because the Court of Appeal is *higher* in the hierarchy than the Crown Court.

Answers on p.141

Things judges can do with precedents

Judges can employ a number of methods of handling ratios:

Following

To 'follow' another case is to apply the same legal principle from an earlier case to a present case because the material facts were the same and the legal principle in the earlier case came from a court higher up the hierarchy or it was an earlier decision of the same court.

Reversing

Here, a court higher up in the hierarchy overturns the decision of a lower court in the **same case**. For example, the Court of Appeal in *Sweet v Parsley* (1969) upheld the decisions of the trial court and the Divisional Court that the appellant was guilty of being concerned in the management of premises used for the purpose of smoking cannabis contrary to **section 5(6)** of the **Dangerous Drugs Act 1965**. However, the House of Lords (UKSC) disagreed and 'reversed' the decision of the Court of Appeal. This can be contrasted with **affirming** where a higher court agrees with the judgment of a lower court on appeal in the same case.

Overruling

Overruling happens when a later court determines that the law in an earlier and different case was wrongly decided. This might occur when a higher court decides that a decision made in an earlier and inferior court is wrong. For example, the House of Lords (UKSC) overruled the commonly held rule that a man could not be guilty of raping his wife in *R v R* (1991). Alternatively, overruling can happen where a court decides that its own earlier decision was wrong and overrules it. For example, in *Murphy v Brentwood District Council* (1991) the House of Lords (UKSC) overruled its own earlier decision in *Anns v Merton London Borough Council* (1978). Furthermore, overruling might also happen where a statute has been enacted which changes the law.

Distinguishing

This is a method which allows a judge to avoid an otherwise binding precedent. It works where the **material facts** of a case are different enough from a previous case (which would normally have to be followed) so as to allow a judge to draw a distinction on the facts. Where this can be done, the judge does not need to follow the previous decision and he/she is said to have 'distinguished' the later case from the earlier case and they can set a fresh precedent.

Relevant pairs of cases which illustrate this method include *Balfour v Balfour* (1919) and *Merritt v Merritt* (1971); *Stilk v Myrick* (1809) and *Williams v Roffey* (1990); *Rylands v Fletcher* (1868) and *Read v Lyons* (1947); *R v Jordan* (1956) and *R v Cheshire* (1991).

In a specific example, *R v Wilson* (1995) distinguished itself from the earlier case of *R v Brown & Others* (1994). Both cases involved the availability of consent as a defence to non-fatal offences against the person. Both cases involved assaults on willing 'victims'. However, in *Wilson* the court took the view that the assaults took place within the context of personal adornment which was allowed where the assaults in *Brown* took place in a sexual context which the court felt should not be allowed. Thus *Wilson* was different to *Brown* and, therefore, not bound by its ruling.

Now test yourself

Tested ☐

Identify the method for handling ratios in the following instances.

10	The UKSC uses the Practice Statement to overturn one of its own previous decisions.	Following
		~~Overruling~~ (circled)
		Distinguishing
		Reversing
11	The Family Division of the High Court decides not to follow one of its own earlier decisions on consent in medical cases because the earlier case involved adults and this one involves children.	Following
		Overruling
		Distinguishing (circled)
		Reversing
12	The Court of Appeal is dealing with a case on the new law of loss of control. The UKSC clarified the law in this matter in a similar case it heard shortly after the new law was passed six months ago and the Court of Appeal decide to apply the same principle.	Following (circled)
		Overruling
		Distinguishing
		Reversing
13	The Court of Appeal overturns a guilty verdict in a case on appeal from the Crown Court as they disagree with the law applied by the trial judge.	Following
		Overruling
		Distinguishing
		Reversing (circled)

Answers on p.141

Exam tip

There is a lot of ground to cover in a question like this. Whilst both depth and breadth are rewarded, it would be best to try and cover the breadth of such a broad question. Read the question carefully to make sure you focus on the correct area. Candidates will ideally need to have covered a definition, the court hierarchy, law reporting, parts of a judgment (*ratio* and *obiter*), types of precedent, methods of handling judgments and exceptions. Also, including examples will often be required for access to the highest mark levels.

Typical mistake

The most common mistake made in this area is including AO2 discussion (often at the expense of giving more AO1 detail), which does not score marks in a) and c (i) questions.

Exam practice

a) Source A at line 1 refers to *stare decisis*.

Describe the concept of *stare decisis* using the Sources and other cases to illustrate your answer. **[15 marks]**

G152 May 2012

Answers and quick quizzes online

Online ☐

Advantages and disadvantages of the system of precedent

Advantages	Disadvantages
The main advantage of a system of precedent is that it provides certainty, predictability and consistency. This was the motivation behind the strict approach to precedent in the House of Lords taken in **London Street Tramways** (below). This certainty allows people to plan their affairs with prior knowledge of the consequences, creates a stable environment in which to plan business affairs and make contracts and allows lawyers to accurately forecast the likely outcome of legal action.	The main disadvantage of a strict adherence to precedent is that it would not allow the law to develop in response to economic, social, technological and other advances. Cases such as **R v R (1991)** demonstrate the way a bad precedent can become perpetuated.
Precedent does have some flexibility within it. Exceptions in the UKSC and the Court of Appeal, as well as distinguishing, overruling and reversing, allow judges some discretion and enough discretion to develop the law to meet changing conditions.	Some critics would argue that any flexibility opens the potential for judicial law-making and this goes against the doctrines of Separation of Powers and Supremacy of Parliament, as well as being undemocratic since judges are not elected or answerable for their actions.
Since our system of precedent is so well established and dates back hundreds of years, we have built up a huge body of law. Decisions and principles have been refined and tested and the law has become settled, precise and predictable. Precedents are readily available and lawyers and their clients are saved time and money in not having to argue cases from scratch.	Having such a large body of law can, however, cause problems: with hundreds of thousands of reported cases it can prove difficult to find relevant precedents. Recently, the advent of computerised databases has helped but it can still prove difficult. With so many finely distinguished cases it can also make the law complex and pedantic. To add to this, the judgments themselves can sometimes be long and complex with no clear distinction between *obiter* and *ratio* (**Dodd's Case (1973)**).

Exam practice

c) (ii) Discuss the advantages and disadvantages of the doctrine of precedent.   **[15 marks]**

G152 May 2011

Answers and quick quizzes online

Online

Exam tip

The key to doing well in c (ii) questions like this is to try and present as many of your points as possible as well-developed points. A well-developed point will move a limited point on and then consider a counter-point or further development as illustrated in the example below:

Point	Developed point	Well-developed point
An advantage of precedent is that it creates certainty in the law.		
An advantage of precedent is that it creates certainty in the law.	As a consequence, individuals are able to plan their affairs in the knowledge of the consequences and lawyers are able to advise their clients of likely outcomes in cases.	
An advantage of precedent is that it creates certainty in the law.	As a consequence, individuals are able to plan their affairs in the knowledge of the consequences and lawyers are able to advise their clients of likely outcomes in cases.	However, some would argue that the price we pay for this certainty is a lack of flexibility and that the law is sometimes slow to develop and alter to meet changing circumstances, as illustrated in the case of rape within marriage (**R v R (1991)**).

Law-making potential

As stated above, the law must change to adapt to new circumstances. If the law were never to change we would still have laws against witchcraft, homosexuality would still be a crime, women would not have the right to vote and we would have no laws to deal with computers and other new technologies. Many changes are brought about by Parliament enacting new legislation. However, in a rigid system of precedent case law would be slow to change if there were not a degree of flexibility in the system.

Precedent has a degree of flexibility by virtue of the limited powers in both the UKSC and the Court of Appeal to overrule their own previous decisions in limited circumstances.

The UKSC (formerly the House of Lords) and the Practice Statement 1966

- Before 1898 the House of Lords was free to overrule its own previous decisions where it saw fit to do so in the interests of flexibility.

- However, in *London Street Tramways* (1898), the House of Lords decided that it would always follow its own previous decisions in the interests of maintaining certainty in the law.

- The problem with such a rigid system is that the law can never change.

- As society did change (especially following two World Wars), the House of Lords recognised that they needed more flexibility so in 1966 they issued the Practice Statement.

- The Practice Statement allows the House of Lords to overrule its own previous decisions 'where it appears right to do so' but cautions against using it too readily – especially in areas where the law needs to be stable and certain like criminal law and areas affecting financial affairs like contract law.

- The House of Lords was reluctant to use the Practice Statement at first and although it has been used rarely, it has been used in areas such as crime (*Shivpuri* (1986) overruling *Anderton v Ryan* (1985) where an obvious error had been made and needed correcting) and contract law (*Miliangos v George Frank Textiles* (1976) overruling *Re United Railways of the Havana* (1961) regarding the award of damages in Sterling).

- The judicial functions of the House of Lords were transferred to the UK Supreme Court (UKSC) in 2009 and Practice Directions 3 & 4 as well as the 2010 case of *Austin v Southwark LBC* make it clear that the Practice Statement continues to apply in the UKSC.

- Relevant pairs of Practice Statement cases include:
  - *Conway v Rimmer* (1968) overruling *Duncan v Camel Laird* (1942)
  - *Herrington v BR Board* (1972) overruling *Addie v Dumbreck* (1929)
  - *Miliangos v George Frank Textiles* (1976) overruling *Re United Railways of the Havana* (1961)
  - *Shivpuri* (1986) overruling *Anderton v Ryan* (1985)
  - *R v Howe* (1987) overruling *DPP v Lynch* (1975)
  - *Murphy v Brentwood DC* (1990) overruling *Anns v Merton LBC* (1978)

- *Pepper v Hart* (1993) overruling *Davis v Johnson* (1979)
- *Arthur JS Hall v Simons* (2002) overruling *Rondel v Worsley* (1969)
- *R v G and R* (2003) overruling *Caldwell* (1982)
- *Horton v Sadler* (2006) overruling *Walkley v Precision Forgings* (1979)
- *A v Hoare* (2008) overruling *Stubbings v Webb* (1993).

Criticisms of the use of the Practice Statement

- The first use of the Practice Statement came in 1968 – even then it concerned a technical point relating to discovery of documents (*Conway v Rimmer* (1968)).

- The first major use was in *Herrington v BRB* (1972) in recognition of changing social and physical conditions.

- Early reluctance to use the Practice Statement was still in evidence in 1973 as seen in the speech by Lord Reid in *Knuller v DPP* (1973).

- However, in 1976 the House of Lords was prepared to use the Practice Statement in the area of contract law despite the Practice Statement's clear warning of caution in this area (*Miliangos v George Frank Textiles* (1976)).

- Even so, it was 20 years before the Practice Statement was first used in a criminal case (*R v Shivpuri* (1986)) where the House recognised they had made a mistake in the earlier decision (only a year before) and that it needed correcting.

- During the period from 1966 to 1980 the House of Lords had 29 opportunities to overrule but they actually overruled in just 8 cases, whereas at least one of the judges in the House of Lords was prepared to overrule previous precedent in another 10 cases.

- The landmark case of *Pepper v Hart* (1993) which overruled *Davis v Johnson* (1979) regarding the use of *Hansard* as an extrinsic aid should also be noted for its significant constitutional implications.

- On the other hand, in cases such as *C v DPP* (1995) the House of Lords declined to use the Practice Statement for fear of being accused of judicial law-making.

- In the recent case of *Austin v Southwark LBC* (2010) Lord Hope adopted a cautious attitude towards using the Practice Statement – he was clearly very conscious of the unsettling effect overruling would have in that case.

- Reviewing the Practice Statement cases, the likely influences for change include changing social and economic climate, justice in individual cases, proper development of the law and the special need for certainty in criminal cases.

Exam tip

In questions dealing with the use of the Practice Statement, higher marks will be achieved by using pairs of cases which illustrate the use of the Practice Statement in particular areas and what motivated its use. This is especially the case where crime and contract are concerned as the Practice Statement said it would be cautious here.

The Court of Appeal

The Practice Statement only applies to the UKSC. The Court of Appeal does not have its own Practice Statement and is bound by the CJEU, the UKSC and, generally, by its own previous decisions. The two divisions of the Court of Appeal do not bind each other although they may be persuasive upon each other (*R v Ireland and R v Burstow* (1998), *Re A (conjoined twins)* (2001)). However, there are a limited number of recognised circumstances where the Court of Appeal does have some flexibility regarding its own previous decisions and those which would normally bind it.

- In the important case of *Young v Bristol Aeroplane* (1944), the court set out **three** circumstances where the court is not bound by its own previous decisions:

  - Where a previous decision of the Court of Appeal has been impliedly or expressly overruled by the House of Lords (UKSC) then they must follow the House of Lords (UKSC) – *Family Housing Association v Jones* (1990) contrast with *Iqbal v Whipps Cross University Hospital NHS Trust* (2007).

  - If there are two conflicting decisions (of the Court of Appeal) they can choose between them as in *Tiverton Estates Ltd v Wearwell Ltd* (1974) avoiding *Law v Jones* (1974), see also *Fisher v Ruislip-Northwood Urban District Council* (1945), *Starmark Enterprises v CPL Enterprises* (2001).

  - If the decision is made *per incuriam* as in *Royal Bank of Scotland v Etridge (No 2)* (1998) refusing to follow *Royal Bank of Scotland v Etridge (No 1)* (1997), see also *Williams v Fawcett* (1985), *Morelle v Wakeling* (1955).

- Also, due to the liberty of the individual being at stake, the Criminal Division of the Court of Appeal has an additional power to those set out in *Young*. This allows them to overrule a previous decision where it appears that the law has been misapplied or misunderstood as seen in *R v Taylor* (1950), *R v Gould* (1969), *R v Simpson* (2003), *R v Rowe* (2007).

- As stated above, it has been made clear that the Court of Appeal cannot ignore a UKSC decision where it appears to conflict with a subsequent ECtHR decision (*Kay v Lambeth LBC* (2006); *Leeds City Council v Price* (2006)) but it **would** be free to overrule *its own* previous decisions where these conflict with more recent ECtHR pronouncements *R (on the application of RJM) v Secretary of State for Work and Pensions* (2009).

- However, the Court of Appeal can, when interpreting domestic legislation, effectively overrule a House of Lords decision which was decided before the **Human Rights Act** came into force and is in conflict with the ECHR (*Mendoza v Ghaidan* (2002)).

- Furthermore, the Court of Appeal has the power to refuse to follow a UKSC decision that has been overruled by the ECJ – *Sharp v Caledonia Group Services Ltd* (2005) due to the obligations under the **Treaty of Rome (1957)** (as amended) and **s 3** of the **European Communities Act (1972)**.

- *Actavis UK Ltd v Merck & Co Inc* (2008), a patent infringement case, created another exception to the rule that the Court of Appeal is bound by its own previous decisions. The new exception is that the Court of Appeal 'is free but not bound to depart from the *ratio decidendi* of its own earlier decision if it is satisfied that the European Patent Office (EPO) Boards of Appeal have formed a settled view of European Patent law which is inconsistent with that earlier decision.'

- Please note above the exceptional circumstances in which the Court of Appeal has ignored apparently binding precedent and followed the JCPC instead.

Historic attempts to free the Court of Appeal from the binding influence of the House of Lords (UKSC)

The Court of Appeal has, in the past, attempted to free itself from the binding influence of what was then the House of Lords. Lord Denning led a campaign to try and achieve the same kind of freedom for the Court of Appeal as that enjoyed by the then House of Lords under the Practice Statement.

- In *Broome v Cassell & Co. Ltd* (1971), Lord Denning refused to follow the earlier decision of the House of Lords in *Rookes v Barnard* (1964), but, on appeal to the House of Lords, he was admonished for so doing.

- Later on in *Schorsch Meier* (1975) he held that he could award damages for breach of contract in a foreign currency even though this went against the House of Lord's decision in *Re United Railways of the Havana & Regla Warehouses Ltd* (1961). The *Schorsch Meier* case did not get appealed to the Lords so they did not get an opportunity to deal with the matter. But, when *Miliangos v George Frank (Textiles) Ltd* (1976) reached the House of Lords on the same issue (having followed *Schorsch Meier* in the Court of Appeal), the House of Lords, despite agreeing with Denning's reasoning and overruling *United Railways*, put Denning firmly in his place on the matter of *stare decisis*, stating that the Court of Appeal must follow the decisions of the House of Lords.

Should the powers of the Court of Appeal be extended?

For	Against
Practically, the Court of Appeal is the final appeal court for most cases as very few cases reach the Supreme Court (House of Lords). If there were an error in the law it could take years to be dealt with **(R v R (1991))**.	There could be a reluctance to use the power similar to the reluctance shown by the Supreme Court (House of Lords).
The Court of Appeal deals with the vast majority of appeals and therefore has more experience and with 37 judges compared to 11 in the UKSC, a broader range of expertise.	Giving the Court of Appeal more power would reduce certainty and predictability. This would be due to there being two conflicting decisions for the lower courts to choose from. Not only would this be difficult for the lower court but it makes giving accurate legal advice difficult.
There would be fewer unnecessary appeals to the UK Supreme Court (House of Lords) if the Court of Appeal had more power.	Giving the Court of Appeal more power would undermine the power and role of the UK Supreme Court (House of Lords).
What is the point of appealing to the Court of Appeal if they have to follow the House of Lords anyway? It would improve the flexibility of the doctrine of precedent if the Court of Appeal had more power.	Giving the Court of Appeal more power would could cause the system of precedent to break down.
It will allow justice to be done more quickly if the Court of Appeal had more power which is partially already recognised by the fact that the Criminal Division does have more power.	Giving the Court of Appeal more power could cause increased appeals to the UKSC.

Exam practice

c)   With reference to Sources A and B (these can be accessed at the URL on page 76):
   (i) Describe the powers of the Court of Appeal within the doctrine of precedent using cases to illustrate your answer. [15 marks]
   (ii) Discuss whether or not the powers of the Court of Appeal within the doctrine of precedent should be extended. [15 marks]
   G152 May 2012

Answers and quick quizzes online

The main reasons for underperformance on these questions were:

In c (i) candidates did not score full marks where they failed to read the question 'what are the powers of the Court of Appeal'. Therefore, answers which dwelt on the fact that the Court of Appeal is bound by the House of Lords (UKSC) and the history of this position were not answering the question.

In c (ii) it was the inability to produce well-developed points which let some candidates down.

Now test yourself

Tested ☐

14 Write one well-developed point about the use of the Practice Statement and one well-developed point arguing why the Court of Appeal should have more power. Use a writing frame to make your development clear.

Answers on p.141

Exam summary

✔ Precedent is a system of law practised in the common law courts where judges follow decisions from previous cases where the material facts are sufficiently similar to the present case.

✔ Precedent promotes certainty, stability, predictability and fairness in the law.

✔ Precedent operates through a hierarchical court system where higher courts bind lower courts.

✔ A system of law reporting exists in order that previous judgments can be identified and followed. Each judgment has a binding legal principle known as the *ratio decidendi* and other legal reasoning and facts known as *obiter dicta*.

✔ Precedents can be original, binding and persuasive. Binding precedents have to be followed but the judge can choose whether to follow a persuasive precedent.

✔ When dealing with precedents judges can follow, overrule, reverse or distinguish. Depending on the circumstances this may allow a judge to avoid an otherwise binding precedent.

✔ There are advantages and disadvantages of a system of precedent but the essential argument is between certainty and flexibility.

✔ In order to avoid undue rigidity, the UKSC has additional flexibility in the form of a Practice Statement which allows them to overrule their own previous decisions where it appears right to do so.

✔ The Court of Appeal has less flexibility than the UKSC but can overrule its own previous decisions in limited circumstances laid down in *Young v Bristol Aeroplane*.

✔ A number of arguments for and against the Court of Appeal having more power have been considered. The essential argument is that the Court of Appeal is, in reality, the main court of final appeal and therefore deserves more power. However, the UKSC has, so far, disagreed.

2 Legislation

Legislation is the United Kingdom's primary source of law. Due to the doctrine of the Supremacy of Parliament, legislation is the highest form of law. It takes the House of Commons, the House of Lords and the Monarch acting together (known as the Queen in Parliament) to create legislation and because of this it is known as an Act of Parliament.

Key terms

The body which makes laws in a state is known as the **legislature**, the laws it produces are known as **legislation** and the activity of making legislation is to **legislate**.

Acts of Parliament

Revised

What you need to know: You need to be able to describe how an Act of Parliament is made, including both the pre-legislative and legislative stages.

Pre-legislative stages

An Act of Parliament starts out as an idea for a new law. These ideas have a variety of sources as described in the final chapter of this unit (below). Wherever the idea for a new law has come from, it will need to be introduced by the Cabinet as a whole following approval and drafting by the relevant Cabinet Committee.

Green Papers

A Green Paper is, essentially, a consultation document. It sets out the idea for a new law and the reasoning behind it. The Minister for the relevant government department will be responsible for the Green Paper which allows for debate and comments on the proposal to be directed to the appropriate Minister.

For example, a new proposal on road traffic laws might be of interest to the police (who will have to enforce it), the legal profession (who will prosecute and defend clients affected), motoring organisations like the AA and RAC (who uphold their members' interests), insurance companies (for any possible impact on premiums) and car manufacturers (who may have to review production or design standards). All of these parties may wish to have their opinions on the new proposal taken into account. As a result, the Minister may need to amend, re-think, re-draft or even scrap his/her idea before going on to the next stage.

White Papers

A White Paper comes after the consultations have taken place and the Minister has made any amendments. A White Paper is a set of firm proposals which are passed to the relevant Cabinet Committee and approved by the whole Cabinet before being passed to Parliamentary draftsmen ready to be formally drafted into a Bill.

Types of Bill

There are three types of Bill:

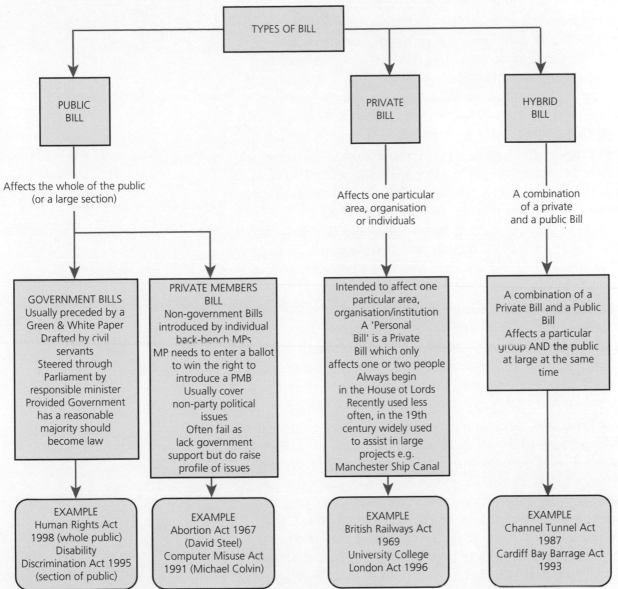

Figure 2.1 Types of Bill

Legislative stages

- A Bill may start in either the House of Commons or the House of Lords (except Finance Bills which must start in the House of Commons).

- **First Reading** – this stage is just a formality to 'announce the Bill' to the House. The title of the Bill is read out and an order for the Bill to be printed is made. If the draft Bill is not ready, a 'dummy' Bill is presented. A date is usually set for the second reading. There is usually no vote and no debate at this stage.

- **Second Reading** – this is the stage for the main debate on the Bill. The Minister or MP responsible describes the aims of the Bill and will field questions. There is a formal debate conducted *via* the Speaker. This is usually a wide-ranging debate which will focus on the larger principles as opposed to specific detail. At the end of the debate a vote will be taken and a majority will be required in order for the Bill to proceed.

- **Committee Stage** – this stage allows for the detailed scrutiny of the Bill. Bills are considered by small committees of between 15 to 60 MPs known as Public Bill Committees. Membership of these committees is proportionate to the number of seats a Party holds in the Commons. Members will often be chosen for their expertise or interest in a particular field. A separate committee is formed for each individual Bill. The committee is entitled to scrutinise every detail and make any amendments necessary for the Bill to reflect the intention discussed in second reading. For an important Bill, it is possible for the whole House to sit as a Committee (e.g. Finance Bills).

- **Report Stage** – after scrutiny by the Committee, they will 'report' back to Parliament – to inform the House of any amendments (if there are no amendments at Committee Stage the Bill can go straight to the next stage). Amendments will be debated and voted on being either accepted or rejected. Further amendments may also be suggested from the House. This stage acts as a safeguard against a small Committee 'hijacking' a Bill and amending it beyond its original purpose.

- **Third Reading** – if approved, the Bill will get its Third Reading. This gives the House a final chance to look at the Bill again as a whole, with all its amendments, and decide whether they want it to go further. The Bill cannot be changed substantially at this stage as it is, more or less, a formality. If there are no challenges to the general theme of the Bill, it will be passed to the other place to start the whole process again.

- **Repeat Process** in the other place (the opposite House to the one the Bill started in) – if the Bill started in the Commons, it will now pass to the Lords (and *vice versa*) to repeat the whole process over again. Any amendments will have to be passed back to the originating House to consider and approve. This can lead to so-called 'ping-pong' between the Houses where a Bill simply gets passed back and forth with no prospect of resolution. This situation can be resolved by the use of the **Parliament Acts 1911** and **1949** which allow the House of Commons to pass legislation without the approval of the House of Lords in certain circumstances. However, this is very rare (**War Crimes Act 1991; European Parliamentary Elections Act 1999; Sexual Offences (Amendment) Act 2000; Hunting Act 2004**).

- **Royal Assent** – this is where the Monarch of the day gives consent and the Bill finally becomes an Act of Parliament. Nowadays this is a mere formality and the Monarch is unlikely to even have the text of the Bill before him/her when assenting. The short title will be read out and assent is automatically given. Although the Monarch retains the theoretical power to withhold assent, no Monarch has done so since Queen Anne in 1707 with the **Scottish Militia Bill**. Her lack of assent was overridden. On the day assent is given, the Bill comes into force at midnight or the date of commencement if specified (e.g. the **Human Rights Act** was passed in 1998 but came into force in 2000).

Mnemonic		What it stands for
I	In	Idea
G	Greek	Green Paper
W	Weddings	White Paper
B	Big	Bill
F	Friendly	First Reading
S	Stavros	Second Reading
C	Comes	Committee Stage
R	Round	Report Stage
O	Offering	'Other place' – repeat process
R	Retsina	Royal Assent

Exam tip

This is a popular exam question. Try and memorise the stages of an Act of Parliament being made by using this mnemonic or making up your own. Close the book and use a blank piece of paper to test yourself.

'**I**n **G**reek **W**eddings **B**ig **F**riendly **S**tavros **C**omes **R**ound **O**ffering **R**etsina'

Now test yourself

Tested ☐

Match the appropriate stage on the left with the correct corresponding descriptive clue on the right.

1	Idea	A. Line by line scrutiny
2	Green Paper	B. White Paper formally drafted
3	White Paper	C. Formal proposals
4	Bill	D. Repeat process
5	First Reading	E. Main debate
6	Second Reading	F. Consultation document
7	Committee Stage	G. Initiative for new law
8	Report Stage	H. Formal announcement
9	'Other place'	I. Monarch approves
10	Royal Assent	J. Firm proposals

Answers on p.141

Delegated legislation

Revised ☐

Delegated legislation is legislation made by some person or body other than Parliament but under the authority of Parliament. Parliament passes an Enabling or Parent Act which authorises the making of delegated legislation.

What you need to know. You need to be able to:

● describe the main reasons why delegated legislation is needed
● describe the main types of delegated legislation
● discuss the advantages and disadvantages of delegated legislation
● describe the controls that can be exercised over delegated legislation
● discuss how effective the controls are
● apply your knowledge of delegated legislation to problem questions.

Reasons for delegating legislative powers

As can be seen from the detail above, passing full UK Public Acts is a lengthy process. In the last ten years Parliament has averaged 35 such Acts a year using the normal legislative process. However, modern life is complex and highly regulated and there simply wouldn't be sufficient time to pass full Acts of Parliament for every area of activity that requires legislative action. As well as saving Parliamentary time, delegated legislation is needed for other reasons. See below.

Key terms

Delegated legislation is also referred to as subordinate legislation or secondary legislation but these all mean the same thing – legislation made by someone other than Parliament but under the authority of Parliament.

Reasons for delegating legislative powers	
Saves time	Delegated legislation does not take up as much of Parliament's time as primary legislation (Acts of Parliament).
Deals with complex issues	Delegated legislation can make use of expertise to deal with issues as wide ranging as scientifically complex safety regulations at nuclear power plants to detailed and technical tax laws.
Quick to amend	Delegated legislation can be altered quickly and easily which allows Parliament to respond to changing conditions such as the recent re-classification of cannabis.
Allows a fast legislative response	Delegated legislation can be passed in a matter of hours in an emergency situation allowing a fast response to things like terrorist attacks or the outbreak of an infectious disease.
It allows for local needs and concerns to be met	Bylaws are a form of 'local' delegated legislation which allow local authorities to make laws specific to local conditions.
Allows for the updating of primary legislation	Primary legislation (Acts of Parliament) can be updated easily to reflect changing standards. For example, sentencing legislation can be updated to increase maximum fine levels.

Types of delegated legislation

You need to be aware of the three main types of delegated legislation. You should be able to say who makes each type, what the effect of each type is, give up to three characteristics of each type and cite a specific example.

Statutory Instruments

Made by: Government Ministers and their Departments

Effect: National in effect

Characteristics: Come in the form of **Regulations (Road Vehicles (Display of Registration Marks) Regulations 2001)**, **Orders (Foot and Mouth Disease Orders)**, **Rules (The Prison Rules 1999)** and **Codes of Practice** (Codes of Practice re: **PACE**).

Can be introduced by negative or affirmative resolutions or through super-affirmative resolutions made by Ministers acting under powers in the **Legislative and Regulatory Reform Act 2006** to make any provision by order if it will remove or reduce a legislative burden.

Statutory Instruments are a major form of law-making with around 3,000 SIs being passed each year.

Example: The **Rights of the Subject, Protection of Freedoms Act 2012 (Relevant Official Records) Order 2012** has changed the law so that historical convictions for consensual gay sex with persons aged 16 or over will be treated as 'spent' and will not show up on criminal records checks.

Note: A recent innovation in delegated legislation has been the **Legislative and Regulatory Reform Act 2006** which gives Ministers powers to make **Legislative Reform Orders** (LRO). These are statutory instruments which remove *any* burdens directly or indirectly resulting from legislation where it would impose: a financial cost; an administrative inconvenience; an obstacle to efficiency, productivity or profitability; or a sanction which affects the carrying on of any lawful activity. An example of an LRO is the **Legislative Reform (Industrial and Provident Societies and Credit Unions) Order 2011**.

Bylaws

Made by: Either local authorities (local town, city and county councils) or public corporations (companies providing services to the public).

Effect: Local in effect or restricted to the provision of a public corporation service.

Characteristics: Local bylaws cover matters of local concern (dogs fouling footpaths; parking restrictions; consumption of alcohol outdoors; harbour regulations, etc.).

Public corporation bylaws cover matters that affect the public using their services (smoking on trains; hose-pipe bans; trespassing near railways, etc.).

Bylaws have to be approved by the relevant government department.

Example: The **Local Government Act 1972** gives local authorities wide-ranging powers to make bylaws and the **South West Trains Limited Railway Bylaws** (made under **s 129** of the **Railways Act 1993**) is an example of a power to make bylaws given to a public corporation.

Orders in Council

Made by: The Queen **and** Privy Council.

Effect: National or local in effect or specific to the activity aimed at.

Characteristics: Usually drafted by a Government Minister then approved by the Queen and three or four Privy Councillors.

Can be used for emergencies under the **Emergency Powers Act 1920** and the **Civil Contingencies Act 2004** (e.g. fuel crisis 2000) and times when Parliament is not sitting.

Also used for transfer of responsibility between government departments, transfer of powers to devolved assemblies (e.g. Wales, Scotland and Northern Ireland) and to extend legislation to former colonies.

Used extensively to give legal effect to EU law under the **European Communities Act 1972**.

Example: Northern Ireland (Restoration of Devolved Powers) Order 2000 made under the **Northern Ireland Act 2000**.

Are the following statements true or false?	True	False
11 Delegated legislation has to be passed by Parliament		
12 Delegated legislation is slow and complex to amend		
13 Government ministers make statutory instruments		
14 Codes of Practice are a type of statutory instrument		
15 There are around 200 statutory instruments passed each year		
16 Orders in Council are made by the Queen		
17 Bylaws could allow your local water company to fine you for using a hosepipe during a ban		
18 Bylaws can be made by local authorities without approval by anyone else		
19 The fastest response to an emergency situation would be a bylaw		
20 If Parliament were not sitting, statutory instruments would be used to bring legislation into force		

Answers on p.141

Exam practice

b) Identify and explain the most suitable type of delegated legislation to implement law in the following situations:

(i) To implement a European Union Directive quickly when Parliament is not sitting. **[5 marks]**

(ii) To allow a government department to issue regulations on education. **[5 marks]**

(iii) For a train company (a public corporation) to implement a ban on the use of mobile phones by passengers. **[5 marks]**

G152 June 2010

Answers and quick quizzes online

Online ☐

Exam tip

The key to these questions is to (i) identify the appropriate **type** of delegated legislation in each case; (ii) explain **why** it is the appropriate type; and (iii) give some **additional** feature, link to the source, example, etc.

Advantages and disadvantages of delegated legislation	
Advantages	**Disadvantages**
Time saving – delegated legislation is quicker to pass and amend than primary legislation.	Parliament lacks the time to properly scrutinise delegated legislation which is not fully debated in Parliament and the opportunity for public objection is lost.
Policy not detail – by allowing delegated legislation to take care of detailed law-making, Parliament is free to focus on producing primary legislation which caters for broader policy aims.	Delegated legislation can be left to junior ministers or civil servants within the department and these people are not accountable to Parliament in the same way as a Minister of State.
Fast – allows a quick response to emergencies such as terrorist attacks, outbreaks of infectious diseases or shortages of vital supplies.	The huge volume (around 3,000 a year) of often complex secondary legislation encourages mistakes and also undermines proper scrutiny, as well as being hard to keep up with.
Expertise – some areas of regulation involve highly technical, scientific and detailed knowledge for which Parliament lacks sufficient expertise.	Whilst it is published, delegated legislation is not publicised as widely as primary legislation – again, denying public involvement and scrutiny.
Controls – there are a number of different controls over delegated legislation which avoid abuse of power.	Some delegated legislation is undemocratic as it is made by unelected persons/bodies and this raises questions of accountability and control.

Control of delegated legislation

Controls over delegated legislation are important for a number of reasons mostly identified above, such as it is made quickly, lacks time for proper scrutiny, is undemocratic where it is made by unelected bodies and lacks the publicity and interest given to primary legislation.

The control over delegated legislation falls to both Parliament and the courts as well as less formal controls like the media, public pressure and occasional inquiries.

Control by Parliament

The Enabling Act:

Parliament may **repeal** the delegated legislation or **amend** it at any time. The Act may lay down strict **requirements, limitations** and **procedures**. **Consultation** is often required with government ministers, experts, interested parties or the public. **Publication** of all SIs is required under **The Statutory Instruments Act 1946**.

Enabling Acts lay down the **nature and scope** of the delegated powers.

Resolution procedures:

Statutory instruments come into force through a resolution procedure:

The **'negative resolution'** procedure involves the instrument being laid before Parliament for a period which is usually 40 days. At the end of this time the instrument will become law unless Parliament has objected in the meantime.

The **'affirmative resolution'** is where Parliament is required to vote its approval of the delegated legislation on a given date during the time it is laid before Parliament.

The **'super-affirmative resolution'** procedure exists to exercise a greater degree of control over delegated legislation known as Legislative Reform Orders (LROs) made under the **Legislative and Regulatory Reform Act 2006** which gives Ministers very wide powers. The procedure requires ministers to have regard to a wide range of recommendations, resolutions and representations.

Scrutiny Committees

Parliament has a number of committees that scrutinise delegated legislation.

Since 1973 the **Joint Select Committee on Statutory Instruments** has the power to draw the attention of both Houses to an instrument on a number of proscribed grounds laid out in the Standing Orders under which it operates (including ensuring that instruments do not: impose a tax or charge, appear to have retrospective effect, appear to have gone beyond the powers given under the enabling legislation or make some unusual or unexpected use of those powers or is unclear or defective in some way).

In 1992 the **House of Lords Delegated Powers Scrutiny Committee** was established to 'keep under constant review the extent to which legislative powers are delegated by Parliament to government ministers'. It also examines all Bills with delegating powers which allow SIs to be made before they begin their passage through the House.

Key terms

Repeal – to remove an old statute which is either out of date, no longer relevant or where its provisions have been subject to a consolidating or codifying act.

Amend – to use a statutory provision to amend a provision in an earlier statute.

In 2003, the **House of Lords Secondary Legislation Scrutiny Committee** (formerly the **Merits Committee**) was set up to consider the policy merits of any statutory instruments or regulations that are subject to parliamentary procedure.

Other specialist committees oversee delegated legislation enacting EU law, local authority bylaws and LROs.

Court controls

Most of the controls above operate during the formation of delegated legislation. Once the delegated legislation is in force it largely falls to the courts to control it. In particular, this role is performed by the Administrative Court which is part of the Queen's Bench Division of the High Court. The court can control delegated legislation through the power of judicial review. Judicial review is a prerogative power (a power which is traditionally exercised at the discretion of the Crown) based on the doctrine of *ultra vires* which means 'beyond their powers'. The process allows the court to determine whether a decision-maker whose decisions affect the public has gone beyond their powers in three categories. Furthermore, the enactment of the **Human Rights Act 1998** has added another area of possible review. See the table below.

> ### Key term
>
> **Ultra vires** is a Latin term which means 'beyond their powers'. It is used in judicial review to indicate where a decision-maker has 'overstepped the mark' and gone beyond his/her powers. The opposite term is **intra vires** meaning 'within their powers'.

Judicial Review			
Review	**Definition**	**Case**	**Issue**
Procedural *ultra vires*	Where the body or individual making the decision has failed to follow some procedure or requirement laid down in the legislation	**Agricultural Training Board v Aylesbury Mushrooms (1972)**	The Minister set up a Training Board without consulting the Mushroom Growers' Association which was a required procedure.
Substantive *ultra vires*	Where the body or individual making the decision has used authorised powers in an unauthorised way	**R v Secretary of State for Education and Employment, ex parte National Union of Teachers (2000)**	The court ruled that a statutory instrument setting conditions for appraisal and access to higher pay for teachers was beyond the powers given to the Minister for Education under the Education Act 1996.
Substantive *ultra vires* for unreasonableness	Where the body or individual making the decision makes a decision which no reasonable body or individual in the same situation would do	**Associated Picture Houses v Wednesbury Corporation (1948)**	A local authority placed a restriction on a cinema's Sunday opening (that no children under 15 would be permitted) which no reasonable local authority would have.
Inconsistency with the Human Rights Act 1998	Where the body or individual making the decision has made a decision which breaches an individual's human rights	**R (Bono) v Harlow DC (2002)**	The defendants were denied the right to a fair trial (Article 6 HRA) when the committee who heard their appeal about housing benefit was found to be insufficiently impartial.

Exam practice

b) Explain in the following situations if there would be a successful judicial review.

   (i) A government minister wishes to repeal an old law. He has not consulted relevant bodies, which are affected by the proposals, before introducing new regulations. **[5 marks]**

   (ii) A government minister is given power to make regulations concerning legal funding. He has now introduced a regulation on immigration. **[5 marks]**

   (iii) A government minister has made regulations which are argued to be unreasonable. **[5 marks]**

     G152 January 2009

Answers and quick quizzes online

Online

The effectiveness of controls over delegated legislation

Parliament

Parliamentary controls are effective because Parliament retains the greatest control that exists over delegated legislation which is the power to revoke, repeal or amend the Enabling Act. This fits in with the doctrine of Parliamentary Supremacy which states that Parliament is the ultimate law-making body.

Parliamentary controls are also effective because Parliament only delegates powers to bodies that are accountable to Parliament and places restrictions on the exercise of delegated powers.

Parliamentary controls are ineffective when considering the sheer volume of instruments Parliament is supposed to consider. Furthermore, the resolution procedures (especially the negative procedure) are weak and rarely used. The scrutiny committees lack the power to amend or reject legislation and are only able to report their findings where and when allowed.

Courts

Court controls are ineffective because judicial review can only happen if someone brings a case. Potential litigants have to establish a sufficient legal interest in the case called *locus standii* and adhere to strict time limits, both of which can prove difficult. Legal Aid is rare and taking cases to the High Court can prove expensive; it takes determination and financial capacity to pursue a case.

Court controls are ineffective because many Enabling Acts grant ministers wide and vaguely detailed powers which are open to wide interpretation. Furthermore, courts can be reluctant to stand up to government due to their belief in the separation of powers.

Court controls are effective as the government accepts the court's findings even when they dislike it. This is due to the adherence to the rule of law. This situation seems to have increased notably since the enactment of the **Human Rights Act** which has significantly empowered the courts in this area.

> **Exam tip**
>
> The key to the exam questions on the previous page is to (i) identify the appropriate **type** of *ultra vires*, (ii) explain why it is the appropriate type, and (iii) cite a case example or give some other extra detail or alternative action.

Exam practice

c) With reference to Source B and your knowledge of delegated legislation:

(i) Describe both the parliamentary and court controls over delegated legislation. **[15 marks]**

(ii) Discuss the effectiveness of both the parliamentary and court controls over delegated legislation. **[15 marks]**

G152 May 2012

Answers and quick quizzes online

Online

> **Exam tip**
>
> The key to doing well with both these questions is to cover **both** Parliament **and** the courts. In c (i) it will not be necessary to have a balanced answer as long as you cover both types of control. In c (ii) it will be important to cover both aspects of both halves of the question – what is the evidence that court controls are effective and ineffective and what is the evidence that parliamentary controls are both effective and ineffective.

Statutory interpretation

What is it?

The methods used by judges when interpreting a word or words in a statute.

What do I need to know?

- Be able to describe the main methods of interpretation illustrating with appropriate cases.
- Be able to discuss the advantages and disadvantages of the main methods of interpretation.
- Be able to describe the rules of language and other aids to interpretation.
- Be able to apply understanding of the rules of interpretation and the rules of language to problem questions.

Why is it necessary?

Often the words of a statute are clear and easy for courts to follow. However, occasionally a word (or words) is difficult to interpret. When this happens, it falls to judges, rather than Parliament, to interpret the correct meaning. This function is known as statutory interpretation.

Common reasons why words need interpretation

Reason for interpretation	Example
Subtleties of language or a broad term – how far should the word be interpreted?	In offences against the person the courts have had to consider how far the term **'harm'** should be extended. Should it be restricted to just physical harm or include psychiatric harm? (**R v Ireland** and **R v Burstow (1997)**).
Ambiguity – where the meaning of a word is open to two alternative meanings or changes in the use of language pose problems.	The word **'gay'** has, arguably, three meanings – historically 'happy', more recently 'homosexual' and even more recently 'daft or silly'.
Technological developments – where the meaning of a word may not stretch to cover the challenges posed by new developments.	In **R v Whitely (1991)** the court had to consider if a computer hacker had caused damage to **'tangible property'** when he deleted files on a computer hard drive. The drive was physically undamaged but harm had clearly been done. The court stretched the meaning by deciding that the magnetic particles on the surface of the disc had been altered.
Changes in the use of language over time – where a word no longer carries its original meaning.	In **Cheeseman v DPP (1990)** the court had to decide what the word **'passenger'** meant in its original 1847 context to determine how it should be applied in the present case – they used a dictionary from the time to assist.
Drafting errors – where a mistake has been made by the parliamentary draftsmen.	In **Fisher v Bell (1960)** it was made clear that Parliament should have used the words **'offering or exposing for sale'** instead of **'offer for sale'** as the latter has a technical meaning which meant no offence had been committed. Parliament had to amend the statute shortly after the case.

The way courts tackle interpretation

When faced with these situations, the judges can resort to a number of rules and other aids to help them:

- Approaches to interpretation
- Rules of language
- Presumptions
- Intrinsic and extrinsic aids.

There are two fundamental approaches to interpretation: the literal approach and the purposive approach. The literal approach is an umbrella term which encompasses three separate rules of interpretation – the literal rule, the golden rule and the mischief rule.

The literal approach

Literal rule

The literal rule consists of giving words their plain, ordinary, grammatical meaning – even if that leads to a ridiculous outcome. According to Lord Esher in *R v Judge of the City of London Court* (1892):

> 'If the words of an Act are clear then you must follow them even though they lead to a manifest absurdity. The court has nothing to do with the question whether the legislature has committed an absurdity.'

The rule can operate simply and effectively for many words especially where the meaning is plain (*R v Bentham* (2005)), but the rule does reflect the traditionalist and narrow view common in 19th century jurisprudence (philosophy of law). Furthermore, whilst the rule does respect the doctrines of Supremacy of Parliament and Separation of Powers, it can produce harsh, unjust, unrealistic and absurd outcomes when applied arbitrarily.

Case 1 – an absurd result

Case: *Cheeseman v DPP* (1990)

Facts: Cheeseman was caught exposing himself to two plain-clothes policemen in a public lavatory and was charged under section 28 of the **Police Town Clauses Act 1847** with 'wilfully and indecently exposing his person in a street to the annoyance of passengers'. The court had to interpret the word 'passengers'. Using the literal rule the court decided that the policemen were not 'passengers' because in 1847 the word literally meant a passer-by and, since the police were stationed there and not passing by, they were not passengers. Cheeseman therefore got away with activity which Parliament clearly meant to criminalise, producing an absurd result.

Case 2 – an unjust result

Case: *London & North Eastern Railway Co v Berriman* (1946)

Facts: Berriman was killed whilst oiling points on a railway line. Under the **Fatal Accidents Act 1864** he should have been given a look-out if he were 'relaying or repairing' the line. However, the court held that oiling the lines was 'maintaining' them not relaying or repairing them, so the Act did not apply and his widow was not entitled to any compensation. A harsh and unjust result!

Case 3 – an unrealistic result

Case: *Whitely v Chappell* (1868)

Facts: In this case the court had to interpret the meaning of the words 'any person entitled to vote' from the **Poor Law Amendment Act 1851**. Whitely had gained an extra vote in an election by pretending to be someone who, whilst still registered on the electoral list, was in fact dead. Since Whitely was impersonating a dead man, he couldn't (on a literal reading) be impersonating 'any person entitled to vote' since dead men can't vote. This is an unrealistic result as it cannot have been Parliament's intention to allow someone to get away with an extra vote (see similarly *Fisher v Bell* (1960)).

Advantages and disadvantages of the literal rule	
Advantages	**Disadvantages**
It respects the theories of Separation of Powers and Supremacy of Parliament by avoiding judges being accused of law-making.	The rule clearly produces absurd, unjust and indefensible results which cannot represent Parliament's true intentions (**Cheeseman v DPP**).
Some judges argue that they are doing Parliament a service by drawing faulty legislation and loopholes to their attention (**Fisher v Bell**).	It ignores the fact that language has its limitations and can change in meaning over time. Thus, words will sometimes have to be given broader context to make sense of them.
Alternative approaches might be unpredictable where the literal rule offers certainty and consistency.	The rule demands standards of unattainable perfection from the parliamentary draftsmen.

The golden rule

Where the literal rule produces an unjust or absurd outcome, it may be possible to escape it by applying the golden rule. This is why it is sometimes referred to as an 'escape route' from the literal rule. It is sometimes referred to as a *modification* of the literal rule with *Grey v Pearson* (1857) stating *'the grammatical and ordinary sense of the words is to be adhered to unless that would lead to some absurdity, repugnance, or inconsistency with the rest of the instrument, in which case the grammatical and ordinary sense of the words may be modified so as to avoid that absurdity and inconsistency, but not farther'*. **Two views** have developed on how far the golden rule should be used.

Where the words of a statute are ambiguous and it is difficult to see which meaning is appropriate, the court may choose between them to achieve a sensible outcome (the **narrow** approach).

Where words have only one meaning but to give them that meaning would be wholly unacceptable, then the court can ignore the plain meaning of the words to avoid the unacceptable outcome (the **wide** approach).

Case 1 – the narrow approach

Case: *R v Allen* (1872)

Facts: Allen was charged with bigamy (having two wives at the same time) and the court had to interpret the meaning of the words 'shall marry' in s 57 of the **Offences Against the Person Act 1861** which states *'Whosoever, being married, shall marry any other person during the lifetime of the former husband or wife (there having been no divorce) ... shall be liable to imprisonment for any term not exceeding seven years'*. The court took the view that words had two possible meanings: 1. 'To become legally married' (which involves a once only change of legal status which Allen has already been through), or 2. 'To go through a marriage ceremony' (which anyone could do more than once). The court chose the latter meaning since no conviction could be secured on the first meaning (*literally* '**nobody**' would ever be convicted of bigamy on this meaning).

Case 2 – the narrow approach

Case: *Adler v George* (1964)

Facts: D was caught inside an RAF base where he was staging a protest. He was charged under s 3 of the **Official Secrets Act 1920** with *'obstructing a member of the armed forces "in the vicinity of" any*

Exam practice answers and quick quizzes at **www.therevisionbutton.co.uk/myrevisionnotes**

prohibited place'. His defence argued that since he was inside the RAF base he could not be 'in the vicinity' as this meant 'near to' when he was, in fact, 'in' the base. The court held that 'in the vicinity of' could mean 'near to' or both 'near to and within' and chose the latter meaning to secure a conviction.

Case 3 – the wide approach

Case: *Re Sigsworth* (1935)

A son had murdered his mother who died intestate (not having made a will). Under the rules of inheritance (**Administration of Justice Act 1925**), the mother's estate would pass to the son as he was her 'issue' (next of kin). There was no ambiguity in the words of the Act here. Sigsworth was clearly her 'issue' but could the court allow a murderer to benefit from his crime? The narrow golden rule is no use here as there is no choice between two meanings. So, the wide golden rule was used to avoid the repugnant situation of the son inheriting. The court effectively re-wrote the Act so that 'issue' would not include murderers.

Advantages and disadvantages of the golden rule	
Advantages	**Disadvantages**
Provides an 'escape route' from the absurd and unjust results produced by the literal rule.	There is no clear guidance about how and when the rule should be used and no definition of what an absurd result is before deciding to avoid it.
By avoiding absurdities and injustices, the golden rule puts Parliament's true intentions into force, closes loopholes and avoids the need to legislate anew.	It is little more than the literal rule and as such is subject to similar criticisms regarding reasonable expectations of the use of language and drafting of legislation.
The rule still respects the constitutional doctrines of Separation of Powers and Supremacy of Parliament by only allowing judges enough freedom to correct errors – they are not deciding what Parliament intended.	Judges can and have effectively re-written statute law which goes against the doctrines of Separation of Powers and Supremacy of Parliament (**Re Sigsworth**).

The mischief rule

This is the oldest of the three rules. It originates from *Heydon's Case* (1584) and involves an examination of the problem with the common law that existed before the statute was passed in an attempt to work out Parliament's intention. The court then gives effect to that intention.

The original case set out four parts to the rule:

- What was the common law before the Act was made?
- What was the mischief that the common law did not provide for?
- What was the remedy proposed by Parliament?
- What was the true reason for that remedy?

Judges then interpret the words in the spirit of giving effect to the remedy.

However, the rule has been usefully re-stated in three parts in *Jones v Wrotham Park Settled Estates* (1980):

- It must be possible to determine precisely the mischief that the Act was intended to remedy.
- It must be apparent that Parliament had failed to deal with the mischief.
- It must be possible to state the additional words that would have been inserted had the omission been drawn to Parliament's attention.

> ### Key terms
>
> In this context '**mischief**' means the problem, harm or wrong in the law before the statute was passed. The word 'remedy' in this context means solution.

Case 1 – the mischief rule

Case: *Corkery v Carpenter* (1951)

Facts: D was found drunk in charge of a bicycle and was charged under the **Licensing Act 1872** which provided that a person in charge of a 'carriage' on the highway could be arrested without a warrant. D argued that a bicycle did not amount to a carriage but the court disagreed, holding that a bicycle was a carriage for the purposes of the Act. The relevant mischief here was that the Act intended to prevent drunken people on the highway with any form of transport in order to maintain public order and safety.

Case 2 – the mischief rule

Case: *Smith v Hughes* (1960)

Facts: Six prostitutes were arrested for trying to attract customers by signalling to men from balconies and windows. They were charged under **s1(1)** of the **Street Offences Act 1959** which states 'it shall be an offence for a common prostitute to loiter or solicit in a street or public place for the purpose of prostitution'. They argued that they were not 'in the street'. However, the court found that the mischief the Act was intended to cover was 'to clean up the streets' and that the kind of activity the prostitutes were engaged in amounted to 'projecting their solicitations to the street'.

Case 3 – the mischief rule

Case: *Royal College of Nurses v DHSS* (1981)

Facts: In this case nurses and midwives wanted to know if they were acting lawfully when assisting with or administering abortions. The issue arose because when the **Abortion Act 1967** first came out, the procedure could only be conducted in a 'surgical' manner and had to be done by doctors. Later improvements meant that an abortion could be induced by hormone drugs (prostaglandin) and this procedure could be initiated by a doctor and subsequently assisted with or carried out by a nurse. Performing an abortion is an offence but the 1967 Act provides a defence to a 'registered medical practitioner'. The question before the court was, therefore, were the nurses 'registered medical practitioners' for the purposes of the 1967 Act? Applying the mischief rule, the majority pointed out that the mischief Parliament sought to remedy in 1967 was the unsatisfactory state of illegal back-street abortions. The broader intention of the Act was, therefore, to widen the grounds for abortion and ensure they were carried out with proper skill and care. As long as the process was initiated by a doctor, the fact that nurses then administered the drug was not unlawful as they were considered to be of the status of 'registered medical practitioners'.

Advantages and disadvantages of the mischief rule	
Advantages	**Disadvantages**
Like the golden rule, the mischief rule helps avoid absurdity and injustice and 'repairs' bad laws quickly.	The rule dates back to the 16th century when there were far fewer Acts of Parliament and those that were passed would have been less complex with intentions that were easier to work out. This makes the rule less suited to the quantity and complexity of modern legislation.
The mischief rule reforms and improves the law as each case is interpreted so as to avoid the mischief behind the Act.	It must be possible to discover the mischief. There will be less extrinsic material (see below) available for older Acts making it difficult to discover why an Act was passed.
Constitutionally some judges would argue that they are respecting Parliament by giving effect to their true intentions, despite using a degree of discretion.	Constitutionally some critics would argue that the mischief rule allows for judicial law-making which is against the doctrines of Separation of Powers and Supremacy of Parliament (**RCN v DHSS**).

The purposive approach

The purposive approach goes beyond the mischief rule in that the court is not just looking to see what the gap was in the old law; the judges are deciding what they believe Parliament meant to achieve. It looks to the spirit rather than the letter of the law and tries to give effect to the wider purpose of the law.

The approach originates in the dissatisfaction with literalism and can be seen clearly expressed in cases such as *Carter v Bradbeer* (1975): *'If one looks back at the actual decisions of this House over the last thirty years one cannot fail to be struck by the evidence of a trend away from the purely literal towards the purposive construction of statutory provisions'*.

The purposive approach received a boost resulting from our membership of the European Union as this is the method used in interpreting European law.

Case 1 – the purposive approach

Case: *Jones v Tower Boot Company* (1997)

Facts: A black employee was abused physically and verbally by some co-workers and sued his employer under the **Race Relations Act 1976**. The tribunal found in favour of the employer because the co-workers had not been acting 'in the course of their employment' (in the strict legal sense [see vicarious liability] – because the employer would clearly not have sanctioned these activities). However, on appeal the Court of Appeal said the Act should be construed according to its broad purpose which was to eliminate discrimination and to compensate victims or punish perpetrators. Jones' employers were liable.

Case 2 – the purposive approach

Case: *R v Registrar-General, ex parte Smith* (1990)

Facts: Smith was a violent murderer who had mental health problems. Having found out that he was adopted, Smith tried to find out the identity of his natural mother which he was entitled to know under the **Adoption Act 1976**. The Registrar General refused. Despite the fact that Smith was entitled to this information under the wording of the Act, the court held that it would be contrary to the purpose of the Act to provide information to someone who might, at some stage, use it to cause harm.

Case 3 – the purposive approach

Case: *R (Quintavalle) v Secretary of State for Health* (2003)

Facts: The court had to decide whether embryos created by cell nuclear replacement (CNR), a form of human cloning using a human egg and a donor's cell, were regulated by the **Human Fertilisation and Embryology Act 1990**. When this Act was passed, an embryo could only be created by fertilisation of an egg by sperm. Initially, the court decided in favour of the applicants (a Pro-Life organisation) that the Act did not apply to CNR embryos and therefore such research could not be licensed by the Human Fertilisation and Embryology Authority (HFEA). However, the House of Lords, using the purposive approach, concluded that CNR embryos were within the same 'genus of facts' as naturally fertilised embryos and allowed the HFEA to licence the research.

Advantages and disadvantages of the purposive approach	
Advantages	**Disadvantages**
The purposive approach gives effect to Parliament's true intentions.	Constitutionally this approach allows the greatest judicial freedom and some critics would argue that it goes directly against the doctrines of Separation of Powers and Supremacy of Parliament.
The rule makes extensive use of extrinsic aids to ensure an accurate and informed view of Parliament's intentions is established.	Like the mischief rule, the purposive approach can only be used if Parliament's intentions can be identified.
It avoids all the absurd, unjust and harsh outcomes of the literal approach and avoids the destructive analysis of language.	Whilst it is suited to the interpretation of European law, it is less suited to the more precise and detailed structure of English legislation.

Now test yourself

Tested ☐

21 Describe a reason why statutory interpretation is necessary, giving a case example to illustrate your answer.

22 Give a definition of the literal rule.

23 Explain what happened in a case where the literal rule produced an unjust outcome.

24 Despite the golden rule having two versions, what do they both have in common?

25 Explain why *Re Sigsworth* is an example of the wide version of the golden rule.

26 Explain what is meant by the terms mischief and remedy in the context of the mischief rule.

27 Which case is the mischief rule thought to originate from?

28 What was the mischief in *Smith v Hughes*?

29 What event significantly increased the use of the purposive approach to statutory interpretation?

30 Explain why the House of Lords in *Quintavalle* thought CNR embryos should be covered by the HFEA.

Answers on pp.141–142

Rules of language

As well as the main approaches to statutory interpretation, there are a number of lesser rules known as the rules of language. These rules tend to analyse the meaning of a word based on the surrounding language and context. There are three such rules:

1 *Expressio unius exclusio alterius* – means 'the mention of one thing excludes others'. Where there is a list of words which is not followed by general words, then the Act applies only to those items in the list. For this reason the rule is sometimes referred to as the specific rule (i.e. the Act only applies to things specifically mentioned or listed).

Case: *Tempest v Kilner* (1846)

Facts: The court had to decide whether the sale of some stocks and shares had to be evidenced in writing to comply with the **Statute of Frauds 1677** which required a contract for the sale of 'goods, wares and merchandise' of more than £10 to be evidenced in writing. Since the list 'goods, wares and merchandise' was not followed by any general words (like 'and other items of value'), it only applied to the specific items listed and stocks and shares were, therefore, not included.

2 *Ejusdem generis* – means 'of the same kind'. Where there is a list of words followed by general words, then the general words are limited to the same kind of items as the specific words. Because the rule focuses on the nature of the general words, it is sometimes referred to as the general rule (i.e. anything included in the general words would have to be 'of the same type' as the specific things listed).

Case: *Powell v Kempton Park Racecourse* (1899)

Facts: The court had to decide whether an outdoor betting ring (known as a 'Tattersall's Ring') would be included under an offence charged as 'keeping a house, office, room or other place for betting'. The general words 'other place for betting' had to be the same type as the specific things 'house, office or room'. Because all the things in the specific list are indoor rooms and the specific thing in question (the ring) was an outside thing, the Act did not apply.

3 *Noscitur a sociis* – means 'a word is known by the company it keeps'. This means that the words must be looked at in context and interpreted accordingly; it involves looking at other words in the same section or at other sections in the Act. Because of this it is sometimes known as the context rule.

Case: *Pengelly v Bell Punch Co Ltd* (1964)

Facts: In this case the court had to decide whether part of a floor used for storage purposes was included in an Act which referred to 'floors, steps, stairs, passages and gangways' needing to be kept clear. Applying *noscitur a sociis*, it was held that because all the other words were related to passageways – that floor used for storage was not included – it was not in the same context.

Presumptions

As well as the approaches to interpretation and the rules of language, the courts may make use of a number of 'presumptions' which are made when interpreting statutes.

For example, there is a legal presumption that the Crown cannot be subject to civil or criminal proceedings unless the statute expressly says it can and that legislation does not apply retrospectively.

One of the most important presumptions is the presumption in favour of *mens rea* (in criminal cases). It means that, unless otherwise stated (a crime which is strict or absolute liability), then it will always be necessary to prove that the accused had the requisite *mens rea* to commit the crime.

Case: *Sweet v Parsley* (1970)

Facts: The defendant let a property out which the tenants used for taking drugs. She was unaware of this activity but was charged and initially convicted of 'being concerned in the management of premises used for drug taking', contrary to **s 5(b)** of the **Dangerous Drugs Act 1965**. However, on appeal, the House of Lords held that she was not guilty as the presumption that *mens rea* (a guilty state of mind – in this case at least her *knowledge*) was required had not been rebutted.

Intrinsic and extrinsic aids

Intrinsic aids

An internal or intrinsic aid is something found within the statute itself which may help a judge to interpret it. These include:

The long and the short titles: The court can consider either. The long title can be used to give clues as to the meaning of words used in the Act. An example is the **Law of Property Act 1925** where the short title gives very little away. The long title is rather more useful in stating that it is, 'An *act to consolidate the enactments relating to Conveyancing and The Law of Property in England and Wales'.*

The preamble: Older statutes may contain a preamble which follows the long title and gives further information about the purpose of the Act (e.g. **The Parliament Act 1911**). These are not common in modern statutes where the long title may be similarly helpful (e.g. **The Theft Act 1968**).

Interpretation sections: Set out lists of what meanings are intended for certain words used elsewhere in the Act and are a relatively modern drafting technique.

Schedules: Provide additional information or appendices to be considered in relation to an Act. For example, **The Postal Services Act 2000** contained a schedule describing the composition and appointment procedures relating to the new Postal Services Commission.

Marginal notes and headings: These are inserted by the draftsman when the Act goes for printing and are intended as a useful reference to aid interpretation. However, where contradictions exist between the actual wording of the statute and the heading or marginal note, the wording of the Act should be adhered to.

Punctuation: Can and should be taken into account by judges in interpreting statutes.

Extrinsic aids

An external or extrinsic aid is something found outside the Act itself which can be helpful in interpreting it.

- Dictionaries are probably the most commonly used external aid because they will define the plain, ordinary meaning of a word. They could be used by a judge adopting any approach including the literal rule where it is particularly useful. Using a dictionary from the appropriate era could prove helpful – *DPP v Cheeseman* (1990).

- Reports of Royal Commissions or law reform bodies such as the Law Commission which led to the passing of the Act.

- Case law appropriate to the area of law.

- **The Human Rights Act 1998.**

- Previous or contemporary Acts of Parliament on similar areas of law.

- The historical setting in which an Act was passed, e.g. *RCN v DHSS* (1981).

- The works of leading academics, e.g. Pollock's definition of consideration in contracts was used in *Dunlop v Selfridge* (1915).

- Reports of International Conventions e.g. *Fothergill v Monarch Airlines* (1980).

- *Hansard* – the official report of what is said during debates in Parliament when a Bill is going through:
  - There was a traditional view that judges should not refer to *Hansard* when interpreting a statute as it may influence them or they might use it in a biased way – this rule was affirmed in *Davis v Johnson* (1979) where Lord Denning was admonished (warned) for doing so.
  - However, in 1992 in the landmark case of *Pepper v Hart*, the House of Lords relaxed the rule and allowed reference to *Hansard*.

- There are, however, certain conditions – it may only be considered if the words of the Act are ambiguous, there is more than one statement relied on and the statements relied on are clear.

Statutory Rules of interpretation

The **Interpretation Act (1978)** is of limited assistance. The Act reminds a judge of some generic rules like: words in singular include the plural (and *vice versa*), words in the male gender include the female (and *vice versa*) and times are in Greenwich Mean Time or British Summer Time (whichever is in force at the time).

Effects of membership of the European Union (EU) on statutory interpretation

Membership of the EU: It is now clear that where a judge is interpreting national law which is in conflict with our obligations under EU law, then they must interpret such provisions in accordance with EU law (*Factortame*).

Human Rights Act 1998: Section 3 of the Act requires statutes to be read and given effect in a way that is compatible with the **European Convention on Human Rights**, so far as it is possible to do so. If a judge decides it is not possible to interpret a statute in accordance with the ECHR, they can make a **section 4 'declaration of incompatibility'**. It is then up to Parliament to amend the law.

Exam summary

- ✔ Legislation is our primary source of law. It is the name given to laws made by the House of Commons, the House of Lords and the Monarch acting together through the legislative process. Try to memorise the stages of the legislative process using the mnemonic IGWBFSCRTOR.

- ✔ Delegated legislation is legislation made by some body or person other than Parliament but under their authority. There are three main types: statutory instruments, bylaws and Orders in Council. The main advantage of delegated legislation is the time and effort it spares Parliament but the key disadvantage is the loss of control.

- ✔ Control over delegated legislation is achieved through both Parliament and the courts. The former uses the Parent Act, scrutiny committees and resolution procedures and the latter uses judicial review and the Human Rights Act. However, these controls have limited effectiveness.

- ✔ The courts are responsible for interpreting the words of a statute. This may be necessary for a variety of reasons such as a broad term, ambiguity, technological advances and changes in the use of language.

- ✔ The courts have two main approaches to interpreting statutes – the literal approach and the purposive approach. The literal approach consists of three rules called the literal rule, the golden rule and the mischief rule. Each rule varies in how much it restricts a judge from straying from a literal interpretation of the word or words being considered. The purposive approach allows the judge to interpret the statute in the spirit of what he or she believes to be Parliament's intention behind the Act.

- ✔ The key arguments regarding statutory interpretation centre on the potential for absurd or unjust results where a strict rule is employed (literal) and the potential for judicial law-making that exists with more liberal approaches (purposive).

- ✔ As well as the rules of interpretation, judges can make use of rules of language, presumptions and intrinsic and extrinsic aids.

3 European Union Law

In 1972 the UK joined what is now known as the European Union and a new, and increasingly important, source of law came into being. The EU is currently made up of 27 Member States which are bound together into a unique economic and political union. The EU's primary achievement has been the establishment of a single market which has the largest GDP (Gross Domestic Product) of any economy in the world. The recent inclusion of a Charter of Fundamental Rights in the Lisbon Treaty has also emphasised the growing social agenda and some would argue that the award of

the Nobel Peace Prize in 2012 has underscored one of the initial aims of the EU – peace in Europe.

What you need to know:

- Be able to describe the role and functions of the EU institutions (especially the Court of Justice).
- Be able to describe the main sources of EU law and their implementation and enforcement.
- Be able to discuss the impact of EU law on the domestic legal system.

Institutions

Revised ☐

In order to achieve its objectives, the EU established a number of institutions under both the founding and amending treaties (see **Article 13 TEC**). The four which you need to know about are the **Council of the**

European Union, the **European Commission**, the **European Parliament** and the **Court of Justice of the European Union**.

Council of the European Union, the European Commission and the European Parliament

The main institutions of the EU are overseen by the Court of Justice of the EU which has the power of legal supervision over all of them (see below)

The Council of the European Union Membership **Article 16(2) TEU** states that 'the Council shall consist of a representative of each member state at ministerial level, who may commit the government of the member state in question and cast its vote'. Membership is, therefore, not fixed. Each member state sends a representative appropriate to the subject-matter on the agenda (e.g. if fishing stocks were under discussion then the Agriculture Minister would attend). Ministers represent the interests of their member state ahead of the interests of the EU. The Presidency is held by each member state in rotation for six months (although the Foreign Ministers have a permanent Chairperson). **Role & functions:** **Article 202 EC Treaty** states that its task is 'to ensure the objectives of the Treaties are obtained'. To help achieve this the Council: • passes EU laws as the principal decision-making body of the EU • coordinates the broad economic policies of EU member states • signs agreements between the EU and other countries • approves the annual EU budget • develops the EU's foreign and defence policies. Since the Council is not a permanent body, it is assisted by a body of permanent representatives (effectively civil servants) known as COREPER. **Key Issue:** Since the Council is the principal decision-making body, its voting methods are important to understand. For most matters they use a weighted voting system called **Qualified Majority Voting (QMV)**. Member states are given a number of votes based mainly on the size of their population: Germany, France, Italy and the United Kingdom (29 votes), Spain and Poland (27), Romania (14), Netherlands (13), Belgium, Czech Republic, Greece, Hungary and Portugal (12), Austria, Bulgaria and Sweden (10), Denmark, Ireland, Lithuania, Slovakia and Finland (7), Cyprus, Estonia, Latvia, Luxembourg and Slovenia (4) and Malta (3) which makes a potential total of 345. A QMV is reached when a majority of member states agree (possibly as high as two-thirds) and 255/345 votes are cast. This stops power blocs and individual member states or small coalitions joining together to undermine policies and laws which are in the interest of the majority. For some matters **unanimity** or a **simple majority** are used.	**The Commission Membership** There are 27 Commissioners – one per member state. They are appointed for a renewable five year term. A President is appointed by the European Council. Commissioners are appointed by the European Council in agreement with the President. The appointment of all Commissioners including the President is subject to the approval of the Parliament. Commissioners are not elected and are, therefore, accountable to the European Parliament who can veto their appointment or dismiss them by a vote of censure. Each Commissioner is assigned an area of responsibility by the President (such as Transport, Health, the Environment and Finance) and are independent of their member state – putting the interests of the EU first. **Role & functions** The powers of the Commission are set out in **Article 17(1) TEU** (and **9D EU Treaty**) and are (mainly) to formulate legislative proposals and to implement and enforce measures adopted by the institutions. The Commission represents the interests of the EU as a whole. The Commission: • has a key role in proposing legislation – it has the 'right of initiative' • helps enforce EU Law in their role as 'guardian of the treaties' (they can investigate alleged breaches of EU law and refer them to the CJEU under **Article 258 TEU**) • negotiates on the EU's behalf with other nations • plays a key role regarding the implementation of EU policy and budget. Around 25,000 members of staff (the EU civil service) work in the Commission in departments known as Directorates-General – each responsible for a particular policy area and is headed by a Director General who reports directly to the President.	**European Parliament Membership** There are 754 MEPs directly elected by 500 million EU citizens across 27 member states. Elections take place every five yerars – the term for which they are elected. The number of MEPs per member state is based on the population of the member states and can be anywhere between 6 and 96. A President is elected in a secret ballot and appointed for a (renewable) period of two-and-a-half years. He/she is assisted by 15 Vice Presidents. MEPs sit in political groupings rather than by member state. **Role & functions** The Parliament has three roles: • debating and passing European laws, with the Council (see below) • scrutinising other EU institutions, particularly the Commission, to make sure they are working democratically • debating and adopting the EU's budget, with the Council. It meets once a month and its 'sittings' can last up to a week. Unlike domestic parliaments it has no 'direct' law-making powers but has a significant role in making law (including the power of veto in some circumstances) along with the Council of the EU.

Figure 3.1 The main institutions of the EU

Exam practice answers and quick quizzes at **www.therevisionbutton.co.uk/myrevisionnotes**

Legislative functions of the institutions

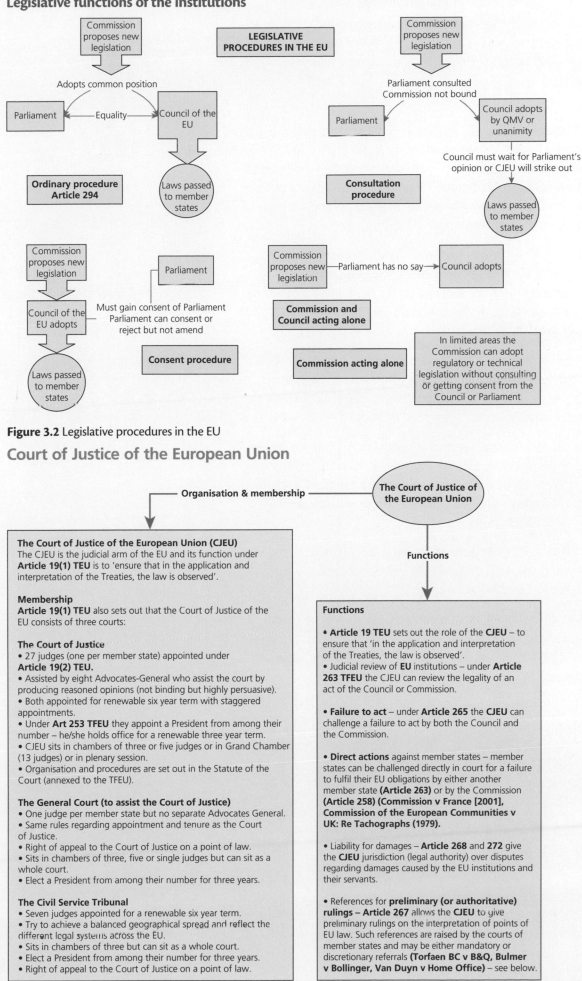

Figure 3.2 Legislative procedures in the EU

Court of Justice of the European Union

The Court of Justice of the European Union

Organisation & membership

The Court of Justice of the European Union (CJEU)
The CJEU is the judicial arm of the EU and its function under **Article 19(1) TEU** is to 'ensure that in the application and interpretation of the Treaties, the law is observed'.

Membership
Article 19(1) TEU also sets out that the Court of Justice of the EU consists of three courts:

The Court of Justice
• 27 judges (one per member state) appointed under **Article 19(2) TEU.**
• Assisted by eight Advocates-General who assist the court by producing reasoned opinions (not binding but highly persuasive).
• Both appointed for renewable six year term with staggered appointments.
• Under **Art 253 TFEU** they appoint a President from among their number – he/she holds office for a renewable three year term.
• CJEU sits in chambers of three or five judges or in Grand Chamber (13 judges) or in plenary session.
• Organisation and procedures are set out in the Statute of the Court (annexed to the TFEU).

The General Court (to assist the Court of Justice)
• One judge per member state but no separate Advocates General.
• Same rules regarding appointment and tenure as the Court of Justice.
• Right of appeal to the Court of Justice on a point of law.
• Sits in chambers of three, five or single judges but can sit as a whole court.
• Elect a President from among their number for three years.

The Civil Service Tribunal
• Seven judges appointed for a renewable six year term.
• Try to achieve a balanced geographical spread and reflect the different legal systems across the EU.
• Sits in chambers of three but can sit as a whole court.
• Elect a President from among their number for three years.
• Right of appeal to the Court of Justice on a point of law.

Functions

Functions

• **Article 19 TEU** sets out the role of the **CJEU** – to ensure that 'in the application and interpretation of the Treaties, the law is observed'.
• Judicial review of **EU** institutions – under **Article 263 TFEU** the CJEU can review the legality of an act of the Council or Commission.

• **Failure to act** – under **Article 265** the **CJEU** can challenge a failure to act by both the Council and the Commission.

• **Direct actions** against member states – member states can be challenged directly in court for a failure to fulfil their EU obligations by either another member state **(Article 263)** or by the Commission **(Article 258) (Commission v France [2001], Commission of the European Communities v UK: Re Tachographs (1979).**

• Liability for damages – **Article 268** and **272** give the **CJEU** jurisdiction (legal authority) over disputes regarding damages caused by the EU institutions and their servants.

• References for **preliminary (or authoritative) rulings** – **Article 267** allows the **CJEU** to give preliminary rulings on the interpretation of points of EU law. Such references are raised by the courts of member states and may be either mandatory or discretionary referrals **(Torfaen BC v B&Q, Bulmer v Bollinger, Van Duyn v Home Office)** – see below.

Figure 3.3 Court of Justice of the EU

Article 267 References for a preliminary ruling

These are one of the most important functions of the court. In 2011, there were 423 references for a preliminary ruling, out of a total of 688 new cases (preliminary rulings therefore amount to more than 60% of the Court's caseload).

What is it?

Article 267 TFEU enables the ECJ to perform part of its supervisory role by giving it the jurisdiction (legal authority) to give preliminary rulings concerning the interpretation of the Treaties and the validity and interpretation of acts of the institutions (i.e. secondary EU Law). In other words it allows the court to hear applications from courts and tribunals of Member States over the interpretation of EU law.

Article 267 allows for two kinds of referral – one where any court or tribunal 'may' make a reference on a point of EU Law (called a **discretionary referral**); and one where a court or tribunal (from whose decision there is no appeal) is involved, where a referral 'must' be made to the ECJ (called a **mandatory referral**).

In the English legal system, any court (or tribunal) from the Magistrates' Court to the Court of Appeal 'could' make a discretionary referral but if a case came up in the UKSC, they would 'have to make' a mandatory referral (because there is no appeal from their decision).

A case example of a discretionary referral from an English court is *Torfaen Borough Council v B & Q* (1990) and the first referral from an English court was *Van Duyn v Home Office* (1974). An example of a mandatory referral would be either *R v Secretary of State for Transport ex p Factortame (No.2)* (1991) or *Bulmer v Bollinger* (1974).

Guidelines on the use of the **Article 267** referral procedure were laid out by Lord Denning in *Bulmer v Bollinger* (1974) and developed in *Practice Direction (Reference to Court of Justice of the EC)* (1999):

According to Lord Denning's guidelines, referrals should only be made only if a ruling by the ECJ is necessary to enable the English court to give judgment in the case and *necessary* means that the ruling would be conclusive in the case.

Furthermore, the *acte claire* doctrine says that there is no need to make a referral if the point of law is clear and free from doubt as in *CILFIT v Minister of Health* (1982) and the ECJ has ruled that there is no need to refer a point which has already been determined in a previous similar case as in *R v Secretary of State for Employment ex parte Equal Opportunities Commission* (1994).

After it has been made and whilst a referral is in progress

proceedings are suspended in the national court until the ECJ has given its ruling.

Article 267 referrals are **not an appeal**. A case may be decided without reference to the ruling but where it is considered, it is binding and must be taken into account by the national court when reaching its verdict.

Now test yourself

1 What is the membership of the Council of the EU?
2 How long does each Member State hold the Presidency of the Council of the EU?
3 Whose interests do the members of the Council of the EU promote?
4 Why is qualified majority voting used in the Council of the EU?
5 Who appoints the 27 Commissioners?
6 Who are the members of the Commission accountable to?
7 How many support staff assist the Commission?
8 What role in the legislative process do the Commission play?
9 How many MEPs are there?
10 How is it decided how many MEPs each Member State has?
11 What are the seating arrangements in Parliament?
12 What role does Parliament play in the legislative process?
13 How many courts make up the Court of Justice of the EU?
14 Who assists the judges in the CJEU?
15 What function takes up 60% of the court's time?
16 Explain the difference between a mandatory and a discretionary referral.

Answers on p.142

Primary and secondary sources

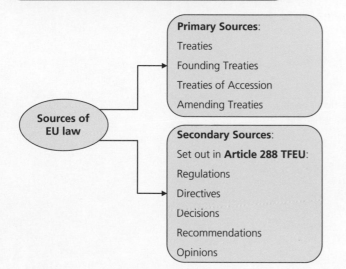

Figure 3.4 Sources of EU law

Primary sources – treaties

The primary sources of EU law are the treaties themselves. These include the 'founding treaties' (that created the EU), 'accession treaties' (that enlarge the EU to include new Member States) and 'amending treaties' (that extended the scope of the EU).

Examples of treaties	
Founding treaties	Treaty of Brussels (1948)
	Treaty of Paris (1951)
	Treaty of Rome (1957)
Treaties of Accession	Each time a new Member State or States join the EU, Treaties of Accession have to be signed: this would be 1973 (Denmark, Ireland and the UK), 1981 (Greece), 1986 (Portugal and Spain), 1995 (Austria, Finland, Sweden), 2004 (Cyprus, the Czech Republic, Estonia, Hungary, Latvia, Lithuania, Malta, Poland, Slovakia and Slovenia), 2007 (Romania and Bulgaria)
Important amending Treaties	The Merger Treaty 1967
	The Schengen Treaty 1985
	The Single European Act 1986
	The Maastricht Treaty 1992
	The Amsterdam Treaty 1997
	The Nice Treaty 2001
	The Lisbon Treaty 2007

Secondary sources

Secondary sources of EU law are provided for under **Article 288 TFEU** which states:

> 'In order to carry out their task and in accordance with the provisions of this Treaty, the European Parliament acting jointly with the Council, the Council and the Commission shall make **regulations** and issue **directives**, take **decisions**, make **recommendations** or deliver **opinions**.
>
> A **regulation** shall have **general application**. It shall be **binding in its entirety** and **directly applicable in all Member States**.
>
> A **directive** shall be **binding, as to the result to be achieved,** upon each **Member State to which it is addressed,** but shall **leave to the national authorities the choice of form and methods.**
>
> A **decision** shall be **binding in its entirety upon those to whom it is addressed.**
>
> **Recommendations and opinions shall have no binding force'**

Because of the lack of legal force with recommendations and opinions, we are only concerned with regulations and directives (decisions have the same legal force as directives except that they can be addressed to individuals as well as States).

Regulations

- Regulations are detailed laws that apply to everyone in all Member States.
- They seek to achieve 'uniformity' of laws across all Member States.
- They are issued under **Article 288 TFEU** which states that they are:
  - directly applicable to all Member States – this means they take immediate effect without further enactment by the Member State (see below); and
  - are binding in their entirety.

Examples include **The Working Time Regulations 1998** or **The Unfair Terms in Consumer Contracts Regulations 1994**.

Exam practice answers and quick quizzes at **www.therevisionbutton.co.uk/myrevisionnotes**

Where there is a conflict between a Regulation and the law of the Member State, the Regulation will apply – *Commission v UK re Tachographs* (1979).

Directives

Directives are harmonising measures – they seek to create legislative uniformity across the EU Member States.

They are instructions to Member States to bring in national laws to comply with the requirements of the directive.

Directives are issued under **Article 288 TFEU** which says:

- the 'form' that the law takes is left to the Member States – in the UK these directives may take the form of an Act of Parliament, a Statutory Instrument or an Order in Council. In other countries, like France, they will amend their national code.
- that Directives are binding as to the result to be achieved (see below).

When a Directive is issued, the Commission gives Member States a time scale within which implementation must take place (often two years).

Thus Directives allow a degree of flexibility and discretion given to Member States.

Example: **The Race Directive 2003.**

Implementation and enforcement of EU law

Revised

Understanding the implementation and enforcement of EU law requires an understanding of the linked doctrines of direct applicability and direct effect.

Concept	Definition
Direct applicability	Provisions of EU Law which take effect in the legal systems of the Member States without the need for further enactment
Direct effect	Provisions of EU Law which give rise to rights or obligations on which individuals may rely before their national courts

Treaty Articles and Regulations are both directly applicable because Treaty Articles became part of our law when we a) signed the Treaty of Accession on joining the EU in 1972 and b) passed the **European Communities Act 1972**. Nothing needs to be done when a new Regulation is passed by the EU – it is automatically part of our domestic law straight away.

Similarly, Treaty Articles and Regulations are both capable of being directly effective. That is to say, capable of giving rights to individuals – provided the law in question does give rise to rights for individuals and that they are sufficiently clear, precise and unconditional.

Directives, on the other hand, are not directly applicable as they require further action to be taken to give them domestic legal force. This is because a Directive is not really a law – it is an instruction (to a Member State) to make a law. Once the legal rights in a Directive have been put into force through domestic laws, then those rights are available in UK courts under normal domestic legislation.

The question which arises, therefore, is what happens when a Directive contains rights for individuals but the Member State fails to enact these rights in domestic legislation? The response to this question from the ECJ has been to develop the doctrine of horizontal and vertical direct effect to extend such rights to certain individuals in certain circumstances.

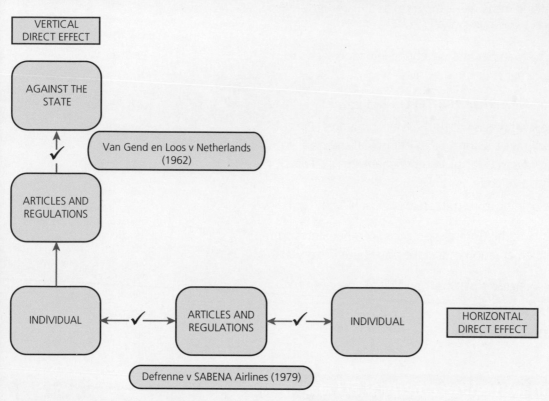

Figure 3.5 Vertical and horizontal direct effect of Treaty Articles and Regulations

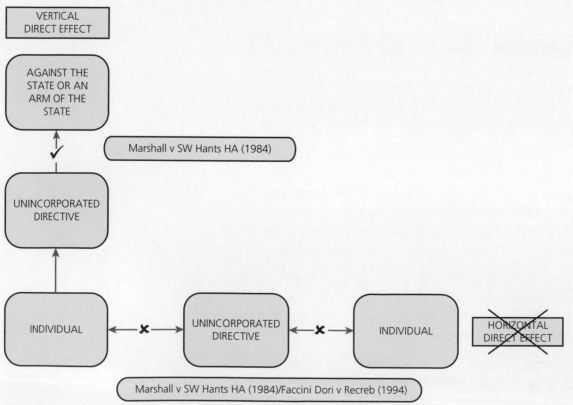

Figure 3.6 Vertical and horizontal direct effect of unincorporated directives

Exam practice answers and quick quizzes at **www.therevisionbutton.co.uk/myrevisionnotes**

Note: The case of *Van Gend en Loos v Nederlandse Administratie der Belastinge* (1962) states that any legal provisions need to be clear, precise, unconditional and must confer rights on individuals before they can give rise to direct effect.

So, Directives can never give rise to horizontal direct effect but they can give rise to vertical direct effect against the State or an arm of the State. This leaves the fairly obvious question of 'what is an arm of the State'? The answer was provided in another British case.

In *Foster v British Gas* (1991), the ECJ set out guidelines:

To be an arm of the State, it had to be …

> 'a body, whatever its legal form, which has been made responsible, pursuant to a measure adopted by the State, for providing a public service under the control of the State and which has for that purpose special powers beyond those which result from the normal rules applicable in relations between individuals'.

In other words, a company that is:

- brought about by statute
- providing a public service
- under State control
- given special powers

will be an arm of the State.

In practice, the test has sometimes had surprising results. Thus, in *Griffin v South West Water* (1995), despite South West Water being a privatised company with shareholders (having been a utility company in public ownership), they were held to be an arm of the State.

The injustice of direct effect

As can be seen above, direct effect works in a potentially unfair way.

Where a Member State has failed to incorporate a Directive on time, individuals in that State are unable to rely on rights in their Member State which other EU citizens enjoy in their Member State simply because of the State's failure. However, the ECJ has tried to reduce/lessen the extent of the unfairness through vertical direct effect and the concept of an arm of the State.

The unfairness of the concept of vertical direct effect is most obvious when it is seen to be giving rights to individuals in some cases and not in others. Two individuals might have identical complaints but one may be able to sue where the other cannot simply because of the random factor of whether he or she works for the state or an arm of the State.

The doctrine also seems to rely on the unreliable assessment of what is the State and what is a private employer. Cases since Foster have proved unpredictable (see *Rolls Royce v Doughty* (1992) and *Duke v GEC Reliance* (1988)).

The ECJ does seem to have acted generously in their interpretations in this area and this is consistent with their reputation for judicial activism (creativity) and the importance attached to ensuring EU legal rights are given sufficient legal force in Member States.

The ECJ has also developed other doctrines to help ameliorate the injustice of both horizontal and vertical direct effect.

The Frankovich principle or State liability

In *Frankovich & Others v Italy* (1991) the ECJ ruled that Member States which had failed to implement Directives were obliged to compensate individuals for loss and damage caused to them as a result. In the absence of any direct authority under the Treaties, the ECJ relied on an interpretation of **Article 4(3) TEU** which says Member States are obliged to fulfil their obligations under the Treaties. Cases will need to meet three requirements: the Directive should entail the grant of rights to individuals; it should be possible to identify the content of those rights on the basis of the provisions of the Directive; and there must be a causal link between the breach of the State's obligation and the loss/damage suffered.

The Von Colson principle or indirect effect

In *Von Colson and Kamann v Land Nordrhein-Westfalenn* (1984) the ECJ developed the doctrine of 'indirect effect'. This offers an alternative remedy to those individuals wishing to sue other individuals in the absence of horizontal direct effect. The ECJ ruled that there was an obligation to interpret 'national legislation' in a way which would be consistent with the objectives of a Directive which the State had either failed to implement or implemented incorrectly. The ECJ relied on **Article 4(3) TEU** as above, as well as **Article 288 TFEU**.

A new doctrine of horizontal direct effect?

In the recent age discrimination case of *Kücükdeveci v Swedex GmbH & Co KG* (2010), the ECJ followed a line of reasoning set out in *Mangold v Helm* (2005) that there is horizontal direct effect in Directives which contain fundamental principles of EU law based on the Charter of Fundamental Rights (in this case non-discrimination based on age). The unusual aspect of this emerging principle is that it creates horizontal rights based on a Directive, whereas the rights in *Von Colson* are based on domestic legislation.

Check your understanding

1 Name two different kinds of Treaty and give an example of each.
2 What is the key difference between a Regulation and a Directive?
3 What is the distinction between direct applicability and direct effect?
4 What do the Foster criteria test for?
5 Explain the main injustice of direct effect.
6 Which key Article do both *Von Colson* and *Frankovich* rely on?

Answers on p.142

The impact of European Union law on domestic legal institutions and law

There are no express statements in the EU Treaties directly asserting supremacy of EU law although several Articles imply supremacy and there is a declaration attached to the Lisbon Treaty asserting primacy of EU law. Similarly, the **European Communities Act 1972** (**ECA**) makes no clear reference to accepting the supremacy of EU law although some sections, again, impliedly accept supremacy. It has been left, therefore, to the courts (both national and EU) to resolve what has been a continually evolving doctrine.

Early EU cases were quite clear in their assertion of EU law. As early as 1963 (before the UK joined) *Van Gend en Loos* established that where there is a conflict between domestic law and EU law, EU law should prevail as the EU had established a new legal order. *Costa v ENEL* (1964) re-asserted supremacy and stated that Member States had pooled some sovereignty to achieve unique and independent legal order. *Internationale Handelsgesellschaft* (1970) went further again by stating that EU law was supreme over the constitutional law of a Member State as well as their ordinary law.

In the UK, judges in early cases saw the duty to give effect to EU law under **s 2 ECA 1972** as largely an obligation of interpretation. In cases such as *Bulmer v Bollinger* (1973) and *Macarthays v Smith* (1979), the courts treated **s 2(1)** as a rule of construction and construed domestic law into harmony with EU law. Lord Denning warned that Parliament would have to repeal **s 2(1) ECA** if it wished to legislate contrary to EU law. The obligation of interpretation approach, however, does not work where there is no domestic legislation to interpret such as where Directives have not been implemented. In such cases, domestic courts accepted the assertion of supremacy laid down in *Marleasing* (1989).

The tension came to a head in the case of *R v Secretary of State for Transport, ex parte Factortame (No 2)* (1990) where a conflict arose between EU law and domestic primary legislation. The House of Lords accepted the ECJ position that such domestic legislation will be considered invalid and set aside. This represents a clear acceptance of the supremacy of EU law.

The extent of the implications for supremacy of EU law are unclear. *Factortame* clearly means that we have accepted a limited suspension of sovereignty for a limited period. The **European Union Act 2011** tries to draw a halt to any further loss of sovereignty by requiring a referendum before the transfer of any further powers. **Section 18** of the Act, the so-called 'Sovereignty Clause', insists, in so many words, that 'what a sovereign Parliament can do, a sovereign Parliament can always undo'. It is a moot point whether this is a realistic possibility or whether the **ECA** has become entrenched and, for all practical purposes, a permanent part of UK law.

Whatever the case, it is clear that the implications, for the time being, are that:

- the UK has another law-making body other than Parliament which is less democratically accountable than Parliament – effectively UK legislation can now be made without reference to Parliament

- parliamentary legislation which is inconsistent with EU law would not be recognised by the ECJ or domestic courts

- interpretation of some UK law now falls outside the domestic courts

- another (superior) court has been added to the domestic hierarchy

- we have pooled or given up some of our sovereignty, challenging the concept of Supremacy of Parliament.

However, some would argue that if the EU's objectives are to be achieved then EU law must prevail. Member States have voluntarily made a permanent transfer of some of their sovereign rights on the understanding that if Member States want the benefit of membership of the EU 'club', they must accept the 'rules of the club'!

Exam practice

a) Source A at lines 13–15 refers to the Council of Ministers and the Commission. Describe the role and composition of both the Council of Ministers and the Commission using Source A and other examples to illustrate your answer. **[15 marks]**

b) Identify and explain the most appropriate source of European Union law in the following situations using Source A:

(i) The EU wishes to alter the Treaty of Rome. **[5 marks]**

(ii) The EU wishes to harmonise the law on banking. **[5 marks]**

(iii) The EU wishes to pass a law on insurance that will be instantly and identically applied in all Member States. **[5 marks]**

c) Source A at line 17 refers to the European Court of Justice (ECJ).

(i) Describe the role and composition of the ECJ using Source A and other examples to illustrate your answer. **[15 marks]**

(ii) Discuss the impact of ECJ decisions on the enforcement of EU legal rights. **[15 marks]**

G152 January 2012

Answers and quick quizzes online

Online

Exam tip

Parts a) and c (i) follow the same format. Candidates will need to cover both role (what they do and how they do it) **and** composition (who are they? how are they appointed? for how long? who assists them?). Role in the legislative process would be important. Using examples would include cases (e.g. *Re Tachographs*) and Articles where appropriate (e.g. **Articles 267/288**).

Part b) – the usual formula applies for all three: a) what is the right source? b) why is it the right source? and c) some further detail such as a case, a treaty Article or a link to the source materials.

Part c (ii): this is a wide question where full marks could be gained through either depth or breadth. Candidates could pick one or two key areas such as direct effect and supremacy and look at these in detail or take a broader approach covering things like **Article 267** referrals, *Foster, Frankovich, Von Colson, Kücükdeveci* as well.

Exam summary

✔ The EU is a supranational community of 27 Member States bound together in a political and economic union intent on promoting peace and prosperity through the establishment of a single market and the promotion of fundamental rights.

✔ The EU will achieve its objectives through a number of institutions central to which are the Commission, the Council, the Parliament and the Court of Justice.

✔ The Commission is the executive arm of the EU and has 27 Commissioners (including a president) who head up a staff of 25,000 civil servants working in Directorates General. The Commission has the right of initiative and proposes most new legislation.

✔ The Council is the principal decision-making body of the EU with the final say on all legislation. They have a revolving membership with ministers representing Member States based on the business on the agenda. They are assisted by a permanent staff called COREPER.

✔ The Parliament is a democratically elected chamber of 754 MEPs from all 27 Member States with numbers of MEPs relative to population. They have a varying role in the legislative process and although they have equality with the Council on the ordinary legislative process, they need only be consulted in other processes.

✔ The CJEU is composed of three courts whose duty is to ensure that EU law is observed by Member States and the institutions. In order to carry out their functions, they have a number of powers including hearing direct applications from institutions, individuals and Member States and hearing applications for preliminary rulings on the interpretation of EU law.

✔ The primary sources of EU law are the Treaties themselves. The secondary sources include regulations and Directives. Regulations are laws that create legislative uniformity and are both directly applicable and directly effective (where they give rights). Directives are legislative harmonising measures and are not directly applicable. Where a Directive has not been implemented, it can have vertical direct effect but not horizontal direct effect.

✔ The lack of direct effect has caused the ECJ to develop ways of limiting the injustice this causes. These include a liberal approach to defining an arm of the State, the concepts of State liability, indirect effect and horizontal direct effect of fundamental rights.

✔ The supremacy of EU law has been established through a number of cases, both domestic and from the EU. The supremacy of EU law has a number of implications for the UK's doctrine of Supremacy of Parliament.

4 Law Reform

The knowledge required in this chapter relates to two key areas:

1 Explaining where the ideas and initiatives for new laws come from.
2 Describing the role, functions and composition of the Law Commission.

Two main skills are needed:

1 Explaining sources of law reform and illustrating these with examples.
2 Discussing the effectiveness of law reform.

Impetus for law reform   Revised ☐

Almost all legislation passed by Parliament is created as a result of proposals put forward by the government or as part of our obligations under EU Law. These proposals for law reform may reach the government from a variety of sources:

Government's own policy – In theory, governments are formed from the party who wins the election with the most votes. That government then has an obligation to put their manifesto promises into action as they have been given a democratic mandate to do so. The Queen's Speech, which starts off each Parliament, outlines the legislation intended to enact these promises. The recent establishment of a coalition government has, no doubt, created tensions regarding the content of the legislative programme but the process remains broadly the same. The **Human Rights Act 1998** is seen by many as a very significant piece of legislation which resulted from a manifesto promise by New Labour to 'Bring Rights Home'.

Obligations under EU Law (and other international treaties) – In 1973 the United Kingdom became a member of the EU by assenting to the **Treaty of Rome** and passing the **European Communities Act 1972**. Since this time, Articles of the Treaties of the EU and Regulations passed by the EU are automatically part of our legal system. Other laws such as Directives are passed to the UK with an obligation to enact domestic legislation to give them legal force; for example, the **Consumer Protection Act 1987**, which was enacted to comply with the **Product Liability Directive (85/374/EEC)**.

Private Members' Bills – These give individual MPs an opportunity to raise issues of concern. These are often non-party political matters, for example, Michael Colvin and David Steel who introduced the **Computer Misuse Act 1991** and the **Abortion Act 1967** respectively.

Social change – The period following World War Two, in particular, saw a great deal of rapid social change with the establishment of a welfare

State. The **National Assistance Act 1948**, for example, abolished the Elizabethan Poor Law system and provided a social safety net for some of the most vulnerable in society.

Moral change – Once again, the period following World War Two has seen a great deal of change. The **Abortion Act of 1967** decriminalised abortion in certain circumstances and homosexuality moved from being unlawful under the **Criminal Law Amendment Act of 1885** to being equivalent to heterosexuality through the **Sexual Offences Act 1967**, the **Criminal Justice and Public Order Act 1994** and the **Sexual Offences (Amendment) Act 2000**.

Changing attitudes to gender, race, age, sexual orientation, religious beliefs and disability – Discrimination in these areas has seen significant legal reform. The **Equality Act 2010** has recently consolidated legislation and now provides a single Act which provides the basis of all anti-discrimination laws.

Public Inquiries – These are often held after there has been some sort of disaster with multiple deaths, although they are often also held to look into areas such as planning and transport issues. The Inquiry is set up by the government who will, consequently, often take legislative action in line with the Inquiry's recommendations. The Cullen Report was an official Inquiry in response to the media pressure and public campaigning (the Snowdrop Campaign) following the Dunblane massacre. This resulted in the **Firearms (Amendment) Act 1997** and the **Firearms (Amendment) (No. 2) Act 1997**, which effectively banned the ownership of handguns in the UK.

Public opinion – Often expressed through the media, has led to legislation such as the **Forced Marriage (Civil Protection) Act 2007** and the **Dangerous Dogs Act 1991**.

Pressure groups – These are formed with the primary purpose of pressuring the government to change the law in a specific area. Some pressure groups, despite having a high profile, have had little or no success in changing the law (e.g. Fathers for Justice). However, others such as the League Against Cruel Sports who campaigned for the **Hunting Act 2004**, and Stonewall who campaigned for the repeal of 'Section 28' of the **Local Government Act 1988** which was included in the **Local Government Act 2003**, have been more successful.

Specific interest groups – For example, the Trades Union Congress (TUC) and the Confederation of British Industry (CBI) who have contributed to changes in employment law such as the **Equal Pay Act 1970**.

Commercial interests can also influence legislative change with the hospitality industry successfully pushing for changes to the licensing laws (**Licensing Act 2003**) and the retail industry similarly pressuring for changes to the Sunday trading laws (**Sunday Trading Act 1994**).

Emergency situations – For example, the response to the potential threat posed by the attack on the US World Trade Center in 2001 which led to the **Anti-Terrorism, Crime and Security Act 2001**.

Judicial decisions – Sometimes a judicial decision in a case may highlight a loophole or fault in the law such as the gaps in the law of theft highlighted by the House of Lords in *R v Preddy* (1996) which led to the passing of the **Theft (Amendment) Act 1996**.

Proposals, wherever they come from in the first place, must be approved by the government through a number of cabinet committees and following necessary consultation. A proposal will then become a Bill and a government minister will have to champion the Bill through the legislative process in Parliament.

Check your understanding

1 What is law reform?

2 Give two typical reasons why it is necessary to reform the law.

3 What resulted from the case of *R v Preddy* (1996)?

4 What has taken three Acts of Parliament between 1967 and 2000 to become legal?

5 Who must give approval before an idea for a new law becomes a Bill?

Answers on p.142

Law reform agencies

Revised

Despite the variety of sources available for ideas for new laws, the government sometimes seek the assistance of expert law reform bodies.

The role of the Law Commission

In 1965 the government set up the Law Commission under the **Law Commission Act 1965** (as amended by the **Law Commission Act 2009**). It is an independent, full-time, permanent law reform body. Their role is to systematically keep all English law under review, to receive and consider proposals for law reform and consult relevant parties and to put forward proposals for reform.

Who are they?

● There are five full-time Commissioners.

● The Chairman is either a High Court or an Appeal Court judge, appointed to the Commission for up to three years.

● The other four Commissioners are experienced judges, barristers, solicitors or teachers of law.

● They are appointed by the Lord Chancellor and Secretary of State for Justice for up to five years, although their appointments may be extended.

● The Commissioners are supported by a Chief Executive and about 20 members of the Government Legal Service, two Parliamentary Counsel (who draft the Bills to reform and consolidate the law), and a number of research assistants.

The functions of the Law Commission		
Function	**Meaning**	**Example**
Repeal	To remove old out-of-date statutes	The **Statute Law (Repeals) Act 1998** repealed over 150 complete Acts of Parliament which were outdated. The **Larceny Act 1916** was repealed by the **Theft Act 1968**.
Consolidation	To draw all the existing provisions currently in several different Acts together in one Act	**Family Law Act 1996**. The long title of the **Employment Rights Act 1996** says that it is 'An Act to **consolidate** enactments relating to employment rights'.
Codification	To bring together all the law (including both legislation and common law) on one topic into one source	The Draft Criminal Code 1985 and the full Code 1989 were an attempt to codify all criminal law.

Now test yourself

Tested ☐

1 A common area of confusion emanates from the distinction between consolidation and codification. There is some useful guidance on the Law Commission's website at **http://lawcommission.justice.gov.uk/index.htm**. Explain, in your own words, the distinction between consolidation and codification. Include examples in your answer.

Answers on p.142

How they do it

- **Referral**: topics may be referred by the Lord Chancellor on behalf of the government, or it may itself select areas in need of reform.

- **Research**: the Commission researches the area of law in need of reform and publishes a consultation paper seeking views on possible reform.

- **Consultation**: a consultation paper will describe the current law, set out the problems and look at options for reform.

- **Proposals for reform**: these will be presented in a report which will also set out the research that led to the conclusions. There will often be a draft Bill attached to the report.

Success of the Law Commission

The Commission has been responsible for many high profile Acts of Parliament such as the **Occupier's Liability Act 1984**, the **Land Registration Act 2002**, the **Fraud Act 2006** and the **Corporate Manslaughter and Corporate Homicide Act 2007** which are all seen as successes.

Other agencies

Royal Commissions are the best example of an *ad hoc* (one-off) committee which is set up to look into a particular area and report its findings and recommendations. The Royal Commission on Criminal Procedures (aka the 'Philips Commission') was set up to look into the law regarding police powers and led to the **Police and Criminal Evidence Act 1984**.

The Criminal Law Revision Committee was a part-time committee, established as a parallel body to the Law Reform Committee in 1959. Its reports led to the **Suicide Act 1961**, as well as the **Theft Act 1968** and the **Theft Act 1978**. It was set up in 1959 but has not been operational since 1985.

Civil servants should also be taken into account when considering 'expert law reform bodies' available to government. Civil servants will have a great deal of expertise within their particular fields and can provide vital, well informed guidance to their respective ministers.

Check your understanding

6   Which Act of Parliament set up the Law Commission?

7   What is the composition of the Law Commission?

8   Name the three key functions of the Law Commission.

9   What are the key stages of the way the Commission works?

10   Name a well-known success of the Law Commission.

Answers on p.142

Criticisms of law reform

Some would argue that Parliament lacks the time for pure law reform as it is constantly driven by routine issues such as financial matters, foreign affairs, taxation, EU law and so on.

Another common argument is that the government has too much influence over the legislative programme and pushing through ambitious party political legislation takes priority over law reform which is not a vote winner.

It is also possible to criticise public opinion and the media. The public may not be fully informed about some matters (e.g. national security) and bowing to public opinion is not always the right thing to do. The media have also been accused of manipulating the news and creating public opinion.

Judicial decisions may alter the law (*R v R* (1990)) or influence Parliament to do so (*Fisher v Bell* (1961)) but there are many who would argue that this is beyond their remit and that judges should merely apply and interpret known law. To do otherwise breaches the Supremacy of Parliament and the Separation of Powers.

Many would argue that in an increasingly globalised and diverse society, greater use of referenda (public votes) should be made to gauge public opinion on matters of ethical and social concern. Parliament, it is submitted, is insufficiently representative.

The role of pressure groups can be criticised. Some groups have taken their campaigns too far in using extreme tactics which then detract from the argument. A lack of objectivity and confusion can also be caused by opposing groups.

The Law Commission has had mixed success rates. In its first ten years it was very successful with 85% of its proposals being made law. In the next ten years however, only 50% of its suggested reforms became law. This lack of success was due to the lack of parliamentary time and the view that technical law reform doesn't win votes. More recently, things have improved and overall, two-thirds of the Law Commission's proposals are enacted.

The Law Commission has, however, had a particular problem with codification of the criminal law with successive governments showing little interest in enacting the Draft Criminal Code. This is also probably due to the lack of parliamentary time and a lack of political will.

In practical terms it is argued that the Law Commission is undermined by poor staffing and budgetary constraints despite being the only full-time law reform body.

> **Typical mistake**
>
> A common mistake in this area is to get AO1 and AO2 mixed up. Candidates who give critical commentary on the effectiveness of law reform in a part a) or c (i) question will receive no credit.

Exam practice

a) Source A refers to the Law Commission.

Describe the role of the Law Commission.   [15 marks]

G152 January 2009

Answers and quick quizzes online

Online ☐

> **Exam tip**
>
> Always try to cover the breadth of the question. Do not assume that the role of the Law Commission is restricted to 'what' they do. Try and include details of who they are and how they carry out their work. Also, including examples will often be required for access to the highest mark levels.

Exam practice

c) With reference to Source A and Source B and your knowledge:

(i) Describe the role of the Law Commission.   [15 marks]

(ii) Discuss the problems encountered by the Law Commission in fulfilling its role.   [15 marks]

G152 June 2010

Answers and quick quizzes online

Online ☐

> **Exam tip**
>
> When the question command states 'with reference to the source(s)' it will be unlikely that candidates can access level four without explicit reference to the source.

Exam summary

- ✔ Law reform is about making new laws or amending existing laws.

- ✔ Law reform is necessary, among other things, in order to deliver government policy and to keep up with changing social and moral standards.

- ✔ Many of the various sources of ideas for new laws can be criticised for, among other things, being lacking in legal expertise, being contradictory or having agendas which lack objectivity.

- ✔ The Law Commission is a full-time, independent and permanent law reform body set up by statute in 1965.

- ✔ The Commission is made up of a chair and four other Commissioners supported by a team of lawyers, researchers and support staff.

- ✔ The Law Commission repeals, consolidates and codifies the law.

- ✔ The Law Commission works by a process of referral, research, consultation and proposal.

- ✔ The success of the Law Commission has varied but they have made some significant contributions to law reform.

- ✔ Besides the Law Commission, there are occasional *ad hoc* law reform bodies known as Royal Commissions.

G151 Answers

Chapter 1

Check your understanding

1 Contract, tort, recovery of land, partnerships, trusts, and inheritance up to £30,000, divorce, bankruptcy, personal injury less than £50,000, small claims, fast track and some multi-track cases.

2 Insolvency, mortgages, trusts, property disputes, copyright and patents, intellectual property and probate disputes.

3 Wardship cases, cases under the Children Act 1989 and other family matters.

4 Commercial Court, Admiralty Court and Technology and Construction Court.

5 Submit N1 Claim Form to court. Defendant given opportunity to admit claim or defend claim. If the defendant defends claim, allocation questionnaire sent to both the parties. Fee paid. From this a track will be allocated.

6 District Judge; County Court.

7 £5,000.

8 30 weeks.

9 District Judge; County Court.

10 A complex case.

11 Circuit Judge; County Court but can be sent to High Court.

Now test yourself

1 Discuss the advantages and disadvantages of using mediation and conciliation rather than using the courts.

(12 marks)

Point	Developed	Well developed
An advantage of both mediation and conciliation is that it is a voluntary method of dealing with an issue. You are not forced to partake.	Both parties have to agree to submit their matter and as a result they are more likely to come to an agreement as they are compromising and in a sense both sides win.	However, the decision is not legally binding therefore there is no pressure to stick to it.
An advantage of using both mediation and conciliation is that it is likely to be a much quicker process than going through the courts.	The courts are well-known for their long-winded process and the time taken to hear cases. Many arbitration cases are heard relatively quickly and often solved at the first hearing.	However, unlike a court hearing there is no guarantee that the matter will be resolved. If there is no agreement the parties may end up going to court adding to the time and expense.
A disadvantage of mediation and conciliation is that a party may not get as much as they deserve as settlements are often lower than those awarded by the court.	In civil courts there will be a winner and loser and the winner will get all the damages and not have to compromise.	However, both mediation and conciliation encourage co-operation and compromise and as a result allows for working and family relationships to continue and allow future dealings.
A disadvantage of mediation and conciliation is that the agreement is not legally binding.	The decision by a judge is binding upon both parties and if one of the parties breaches the agreement it can be enforced by the courts. In mediation and conciliation there is not such security. If one of the parties chooses to ignore the agreement then they are free to do so.	However, nowadays, particularly with separating and divorcing couples, there will be a formal record of the agreement and a signed settlement document making it enforceable.

2 Match the statement with the correct answer.

Statement	Answer
The name given to the methods of dealing with civil matters without going to court	Alternative Dispute Resolution (ADR)
The form of ADR where the third party remains passive	Mediation
The form of ADR where the third party plays an active role in helping the parties come to a compromise	Conciliation
This form of ADR is governed by statute	Arbitration
The name of the Act of Parliament governing arbitration	Arbitration Act
Mediation is particularly helpful when dealing with these sorts of matters	Relationship issues
Conciliation is particularly helpful when dealing with these sorts of matters	Employment disputes
Arbitration is particularly helpful when dealing with these sorts of matters	Commercial issues
An example of a formal method of approaching mediation	Formalised Settlement Conference
An example of a commercial mediation service	The Centre for Effective Dispute Resolution (CEDR)

(Continued)

(Continued)

(Continued)

Statement	Answer
One of the main advantages of all three types of ADR	Privacy
One of the main disadvantages of mediation and conciliation	Lack of binding agreement
The name of the decision made by the arbitrator(s)	Award
A reason arbitration is becoming unpopular	Due to increased delays and costs.
When might mediation not be voluntary	When divorcing and separating couples are referred before being allowed to go to court
An organisation devoted to preventing and resolving employment disputes	Advisory, Conciliation and Arbitration Service (ACAS)

Chapter 2

Now test yourself

1 Police and Criminal Evidence.

2 To stop and search.

3 The police must identify themselves and follow the rules set out in PACE or any search or arrest will not be lawful.

4 It just sets out what cannot be the sole reason for suspicion, personal appearance or previous convictions. It does not define reasonable suspicion.

5 Outer coat, jacket and gloves.

6 To search anyone in a specified area without reasonable suspicion for 24 hours in anticipation of violence.

7 When a person is suspected of being about to commit an offence, in the process of committing an offence or has committed an offence.

8 The Serious Organised Crime and Police Act 2005.

9 An officer can only arrest if s/he has reasonable grounds for believing that it is necessary to make the arrest for one of the following reasons:

- to enable the name and address of suspect to be ascertained
- to prevent the person causing physical injury to himself or any other person
- suffering physical injury
- causing loss or damage to property
- committing an offence against public decency
- causing an unlawful obstruction of the highway
- to protect a child or vulnerable person
- to allow the prompt and effective investigation of the offence or the conduct of the person
- to prevent any prosecution for the offence from being hindered by the disappearance of the person in question.

10 Why they are under arrest, the reason for arrest, why the arrest is necessary and give a caution.

11 Fill in the following grid detailing powers of the police and rights of the individual at the police station.

Powers of the police	Limitations on powers	Individual rights
To detain individuals	Only for certain time limits: 24 hours for any offence; 36 hours for indictable offence with permission of senior officer; 96 hours with permission of magistrates	Custody officer monitors detention – must release if no good reason to detain
Can delay right to legal advice	Only if authorised by senior officer for an indictable offence if reasonable grounds to believe it would lead to interference with evidence or alerting others involved in the offence.	Right to legal advice under s 58 PACE Act – it may only be available over the phone
Can delay right to inform	Only if authorised by senior officer for an indictable offence if reasonable grounds to believe it would lead to interference with evidence or alerting others involved in the offence.	Right to have someone informed of detention under s 56 PACE Act
Can interview suspect	Must be taped and two copies made; Oppression may not be used	Appropriate adult present for young offenders or if mental problems; Interpreter if necessary; Right to a solicitor
Can search suspect using one of three types of search: Check-in search, Strip search, Intimate search	Only if going to find something prohibited; Non-intimate search; Strip search: Only if reasonable suspicion person has an article a person in detention should not have; Intimate search: Only for weapons or class A drugs	Must be done in particular way to protect privacy of suspect: Strip search: In private by same sex officer, keep half clothes on at any one time; Intimate search: By doctor or nurse unless high-ranking officer authorises a police officer to do it in an emergency
Can take samples	Non-intimate: fingerprints, hair from head, fingernails, saliva, swab from mouth etc.	By police; With reasonable force if necessary; permission not required from the suspect
	Intimate: blood, urine, semen, dental impression, swab from anywhere other than the mouth.	By doctor or nurse; With permission from the suspect

Chapter 3

Now test yourself

1 In which court would the following people be likely to be tried and why?

Defendant	Court
Fred has been charged with murder	Crown Court because it is an indictable offence
Sandra has been charged with stealing a large box of chocolates from the local supermarket	Theft is triable either way. The magistrates would decide it was within their jurisdiction so it would probably be in the Magistrates' Court but Sandra could choose a Crown Court trial
Aaron has been charged with driving without insurance	Magistrates' Court as it is a Summary offence
Kyle has been charged with stealing £60,000 from the elderly lady he was caring for	Theft is triable either way but the magistrates would probably decide this was too serious for them to deal with so would send the case to Crown Court for trial
Billy has pleaded guilty to causing actual bodily harm	As Billy has pleaded guilty, there does not need to be a trial. It is a triable-either-way offence so the magistrates could sentence or send to Crown Court for sentencing if they think a more severe sentence is warranted

2 Fill in the following grids.

Bail	
There is a presumption in favour of bail because.....	Everyone is presumed innocent until the contrary is proved
Reasons to refuse bail	**Why this is important**
1. D will fail to surrender to custody	If they do not turn up for trial, this wastes time and money and justice is not served
2. D will commit an offence whilst on bail	There has to be a balance between protecting the public and the presumption in favour of bail so bail may be refused to protect the public from further offences
3. D will interfere with witnesses or otherwise obstruct the course of justice	A fair trial is necessary for justice

(Continued)

4. D should be kept in custody for his own protection or welfare	If the offence is one that causes possible vigilante behaviour e.g. serious offences against children

Factors to consider	Which reason to refuse does this relate to?	Examples
1. The nature and seriousness of the offence	Failure to surrender to custody Custody for own protection or welfare	Serious offence more likely to abscond as high penalties Person suspected of molesting children may be subject to vigilante attacks
2. Defendant's character, record, friends and community ties	Failure to surrender to custody	Those with close ties to the area are less likely to abscond
3. D's record of previous behaviour on bail	Failure to surrender to custody May commit offences on bail May interfere with witnesses	If they have behaved in a particular way on a previous granting of bail, they are more likely to behave in that way again
4. The strength of evidence against D	Failure to surrender to custody	If the evidence is very strong, they are likely to be convicted so may abscond if the penalty is high

Consider the arguments for and against granting bail to each of the following: What conditions, if any, should be attached to bail if it is granted?

Note: These are merely suggested answers.

3 Elizabeth is likely to be granted bail as none of the reasons for refusing bail are likely to apply to her. She is unlikely to fail to surrender due to ties to the area and there is nothing to indicate she would reoffend, interfere with witnesses or need protection from the public. She would probably be given bail on the condition that her passport was handed in.

4 Brian may be refused bail on the grounds that as he lives in a caravan and is unemployed, he may leave the area and fail to surrender to custody. His previous bail record would be looked at to help with the decision. As the offence is not very serious, he may be given bail with a curfew and an electronic tag.

5 As this is a very serious drug dealing case, it is unlikely that Bill would be granted bail. Everything else is in Bill's favour as he has a steady job and good ties to the area. On balance, with a large quantity of heroin found in his car, he is likely to be remanded in custody.

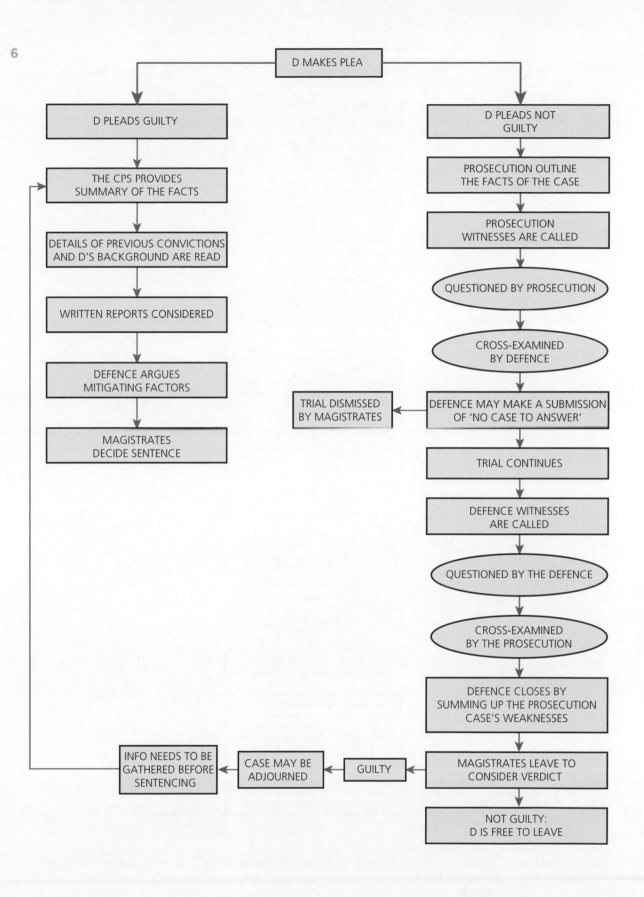

7

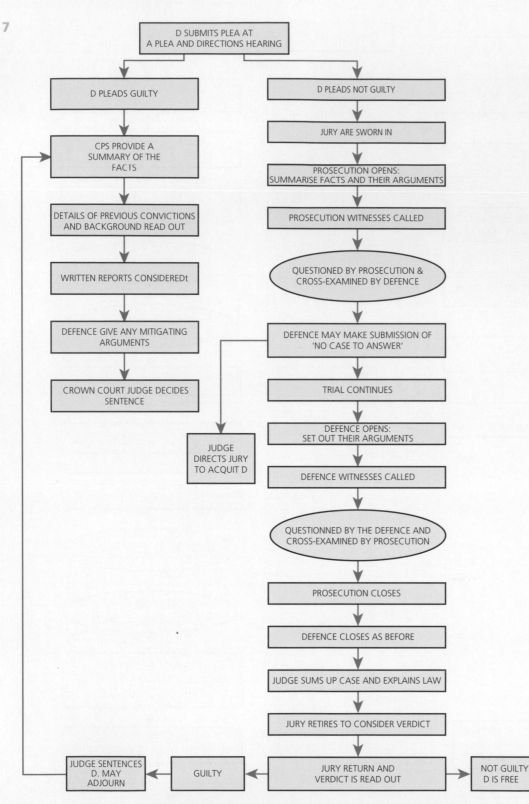

D SUBMITS PLEA AT
A PLEA AND DIRECTIONS HEARING

D PLEADS GUILTY

D PLEADS NOT GUILTY

CPS PROVIDE A
SUMMARY OF THE
FACTS

JURY ARE SWORN IN

PROSECUTION OPENS:
SUMMARISE FACTS AND THEIR ARGUMENTS

DETAILS OF PREVIOUS CONVICTIONS
AND BACKGROUND READ OUT

PROSECUTION WITNESSES CALLED

WRITTEN REPORTS CONSIDEREDt

QUESTIONED BY PROSECUTION &
CROSS-EXAMINED BY DEFENCE

DEFENCE GIVE ANY MITIGATING
ARGUMENTS

DEFENCE MAY MAKE SUBMISSION OF
'NO CASE TO ANSWER'

CROWN COURT JUDGE DECIDES
SENTENCE

TRIAL CONTINUES

JUDGE
DIRECTS JURY
TO ACQUIT D

DEFENCE OPENS:
SET OUT THEIR ARGUMENTS

DEFENCE WITNESSES CALLED

QUESTIONNED BY THE DEFENCE AND
CROSS-EXAMINED BY PROSECUTION

PROSECUTION CLOSES

DEFENCE CLOSES AS BEFORE

JUDGE SUMS UP CASE AND EXPLAINS LAW

JURY RETIRES TO CONSIDER VERDICT

JUDGE SENTENCES
D. MAY
ADJOURN

GUILTY

JURY RETURN AND
VERDICT IS READ OUT

NOT GUILTY
D IS FREE

8 Complete the following table:

Party	Court hearing appeal	Reason/ Grounds for appeal	Nature of appeal/Procedure	Possible outcome
Defendant	Court of Appeal	Conviction	Leave required from a Court of Appeal judge (only 30% get leave). Only ground for appeal is that the conviction was unsafe.	They may confirm conviction, reverse the decision and acquit the defendant or may vary the conviction and find the defendant guilty of a lesser offence May order a retrial

(Continued)

Party	Court hearing appeal	Reason/ Grounds for appeal	Nature of appeal/Procedure	Possible outcome
Defendant	Court of Appeal	Sentence	Leave required from a Court of Appeal judge (only 30% get leave).	Can decrease sentence but not increase it
Defendant	UK Supreme Court		Point of Law of general public importance Permission (leave) must be granted by the Supreme Court or Queen's Bench Division	Decide the point of law which is then applied to the case
Prosecution	High Court	Acquittal	Appeal to the High Court for an order to quash an acquittal because of jury nobbling (Criminal Procedure and Investigations Act 1996)	Retrial ordered
Prosecution	Court of Appeal via Attorney-General	Acquittal (CJA 1972)	AG may refer a point of Law to the CA – (CJA 1972)	They may confirm, overrule or amend the law but the acquittal stands
Prosecution	Court of Appeal via Attorney-General	Sentence (s 36 CJA 1988)	AG may refer an unduly lenient sentence to the CA for review	Sentence may be confirmed or increased
Prosecution	UK Supreme Court		Prosecution have the right to appeal from the Divisional Court or the Court of Appeal to the UK Supreme Court It must involve a point of law of public importance and leave/permission must be given to appeal from the CA or HL Very few cases are appealed to the House of Lords	Decide point of law

9 14 days.
10 Criminal Justice Act 2003.
11 Court of Appeal (Criminal Division).
12 Queen's Bench Divisional Court.
13 An indictment.
14 The jury retires to consider the verdict.
15 The legal right to hear the case.

Chapter 4

Now test yourself

1 Complete the following table with the appropriate names of the aims and the suitable punishments to fulfill those aims using the information given below.

Aim	Description of aim of theory	Suitable punishment
Retribution	Punishment imposed only on grounds that an offence has been committed, with no consideration of the defendant	Tariff sentences Sentence must be proportionate to the crime
Individual deterrence	The offender is deterred through fear of further punishment	Prison sentence Heavy fine
General deterrence	Potential offenders warned as to likely punishment	Long sentence as an example to others
Rehabilitation	Reform offender's behaviour	Individualised sentence Community order
Protection of the public	Offender is made incapable of committing further crime Society is protected from crime	Long prison sentences Curfews with tagging Banning orders
Reparation	Repayment/reparation to victim or to community	Compensation order Unpaid work Reparation schemes
Denunciation	Society expressing its disapproval Reinforces moral boundaries	Publicity Unpaid work Naming and shaming

(Continued)

2 Fill in the table with appropriate sentences available for each age range.

Age category	Custodial sentences	Community sentences	Fines	Discharges	Others
Under 12 (10–11)	Detention at Her Majesty's pleasure	Youth Rehabilitation Order (no unpaid work)	max £250	Discharges	Reprimands and Warnings
Under 14 (12–13)	Detention at Her Majesty's pleasure Detention and training orders	Youth Rehabilitation Order (no unpaid work)	max £250	Discharges	Reprimands and Warnings
Under 16 (14–15)	Detention at Her Majesty's pleasure Detention and training orders	Youth Rehabilitation Order (no unpaid work)	Max £1,000	Discharges	Reprimands and Warnings
Under 18 (16–17)	Detention at Her Majesty's pleasure Detention and training orders	Youth Rehabilitation Order	Max £1,000	Absolute and Conditional Discharges	Reprimands and Warnings
Under 21 (18–20)	Young Offender's Institutions Life sentence Fixed term sentences	Community Order	£5,000 max in Magistrates' Court Unlimited in Crown Court	Absolute and Conditional Discharges	Disqualification from driving
21+	Life sentence Fixed term sentences Extended sentences Indeterminate sentences Home Detention Curfew Suspended sentence	Community Order	£5000 max in Magistrates' Court Unlimited in Crown Court	Absolute and Conditional Discharges	Disqualification from driving

Chapter 5

Now test yourself

1 Fill in the following grid detailing the role of judges in various courts.

Type of judge	How many are there?	Which court/courts do they sit in?	What is their role?
Justices of the Supreme Court	12	UK Supreme Court	Hear appeals on points of law
Lords Justices of Appeal	38	Court of Appeal	Hear appeals: **Criminal** against conviction or sentence **Civil** on fining and/or amount awarded
High Court Judges	110	Divisions of the High Court Crown Court	Sit in one of Divisional courts Hear first instance cases, civil and serious criminal cases in Crown Court
Circuit Judges	665	Crown Court	Try cases in Crown Court with a jury Pass sentence on convicted
Recorders	1155	Crown Court	Try cases in Crown Court with a jury Pass sentence on convicted
District Judges	447 + 754 deputies	County Court	Decide liability and remedy in civil cases Also deal with small claims
District Judges (Magistrates' Court)	141 + 134 deputies	Magistrates' Court	Criminal cases: decide law and verdict, pass sentence

2 Judicial Studies Board

3 70

4 The Tribunals, Courts and Enforcement Act 2007

5 2001

6 2009

7 To hear appeals on points of law

8 1993

9 1988

10 See the completed figure below

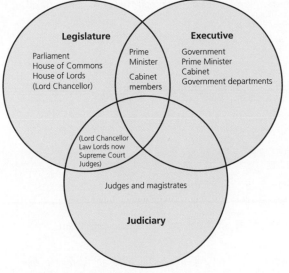

Now test yourself

1 Using the following table, compare the training of solicitors and barristers.

Chapter 6

Check your understanding

1 Obligations including contract, restitution and tort, public law (including constitutional law, administrative law and human rights law), criminal law, property law, equity and the law of trusts, law of the European Union and legal research.

2 Practical based, emphasis on skills such as client-interviewing, negotiation, drafting documents, business management and advocacy.

3 Family and Matrimonial, Criminal, Personal Injury, Wills and Probate, Litigation, etc.

4 A practical course building on the vocational training provided by the LPC.

5 When all aspects of training have been successfully completed.

6 Before undertaking the BPTC.

7 Advocacy and role playing, case preparation, drafting legal documents, opinion writing and interpersonal skills.

8 First six spent shadowing Supervisor; second six pupils can undertake own cases under the supervision of their Supervisor.

9 Following completion of the required qualifying sessions and successful completion of the BPTC.

10 Call themselves a barrister in connection with the supply of legal services.

Training	Solicitors	Barristers
Education – academic	Qualifying law degree – core subjects e.g. public law and criminal law. OR Degree in another subject plus the Common Professional Examination or Graduate Diploma in Law. This course covers the foundation/core topics. May join the profession if Fellow of the Institute of Legal Executives.	Qualifying law degree – core subjects e.g. public law and criminal law. OR Degree in another subject plus the Common Professional Examination or Graduate Diploma in Law. This course covers the foundation/core topics.
Vocational	Undertake one-year Legal Practice Course. Course develops the skills required to practice e.g. client-interviewing, negotiation, drafting documents, business management and advocacy.	Join one of the Inns of Court. Undertake qualifying sessions or attend residential training courses. Undertake the Bar Professional Training Course for one year. The course will develop the skills required for a career at the Bar e.g. advocacy, case preparation, drafting legal documents, opinion-writing (giving written advice on cases) and interpersonal skills. Admitted to the Bar.
Practical	Two-year Training Contract working within at least three different areas of law. Minimum pay outside London is £16,650 per annum. 20 days Professional Skills Course. Admitted to the Roll.	One-year pupillage. First six months shadowing the Supervisor. Second six months pupil able to undertake supervised work of their own. Minimum pay is £12,000 for the year.

Student activity

Possible points for discussion:

Good points about the training:

1 In terms of the Legal Practice Course for solicitors, it is now available in a wide range of institutions including universities.

2 For both practical parts of the training there is now a minimum wage payable.

3 The Inns of Courts have a wide range of bursaries and scholarships available to help students whilst training.

Problems with the training:

1 The costs of both the Legal Practice Course and the Bar Professional Training Course are high.

2 There are far too many people undertaking the vocational courses but very few Training Contracts or Pupillage available.

3 Undertaking the one-year Common Professional Examination or Graduate Diploma in Law may mean that the trainee lacks wide-ranging legal knowledge as the course only lasts one year.

Chapter 7

Check your understanding

1 A person must be:

a) Aged between 18 and 65 on appointment.

b) Live or work near the Local Justice Area they are allocated to.

c) Be prepared to commit to sitting at least 26 half-days per year.

2 There may be situations where the arresting officer or colleagues of his were sitting on the bench trying the defendant. This would be unfair on the defendant.

3 It is felt that a person with a number of minor convictions may lack respect for the law, and the public may lack confidence in them.

4 Personal integrity – respect and trust of others – respect for confidences – absence of any matter which might bring them or the magistracy into disrepute – willingness to be circumspect in private, working and public life (as per Ministry of Justice).

5 Appreciation and acceptance of the rule of law – understanding of society in general – respect for people from different ethnic, cultural or social backgrounds – awareness and understanding of life beyond family, friends and work is highly desirable, as in an understanding of your local community (as per Ministry of Justice).

6 The candidates' potential judicial aptitude.

7 Lord Chancellor.

8 A person must be:

a) Aged between 18 and 70.

b) Registered as a parliamentary or local government elector.

c) Resident in UK for five years since age of 13.

9 Imprisonment or detention for life, detention during Her Majesty's Pleasure, a term of imprisonment or detention of five years or more, sentenced for public protection, extended sentence.

10 10 years.

11 Due to being mentally disordered, cannot sufficiently understand English, suffers a disability that will make the person unsuitable to sit as a jury e.g. deaf.

12 When their commanding officer certifies that they are required for duty.

13 Criminal Justice Act 2003.

Now test yourself

1   Discuss the advantages and disadvantage of using lay magistrates to deal with criminal cases.   **[12 marks]**

Point	Developed	Well developed
An advantage of using lay magistrates in criminal cases is that the magistrates come from the local area and therefore have local knowledge.	This means that they should have awareness of local crime patterns and local opinions as opposed to a District Judge from a different area.	However, now that a person just needs to work in the local justice area it may mean that they know very little about the local community and the problems of the area as they simply come to that place to work.
An advantage of using lay magistrates is that they provide a cross-section of society in terms of gender, ethnic origin, age and social background.	Magistrates are almost exactly balanced for gender, while 71% of District Judges are male. 8% of magistrates come from ethnic minorities as opposed to 3.9% of District Judges (although 6.9% of Deputy District Judges are from ethnic minorities).	However, it is said that magistrates are middle-class and middle-minded. This may be due to the fact that many people who are not in this socio-economic category cannot afford to take on the role.
A disadvantage of using lay magistrates is that they lack any formal legal qualifications.	There are no academic qualifications required, only qualities. As a result of this lack of knowledge, some magistrates are known to rely too heavily on the legal clerk for advice.	However, with the introduction of MNTI2 the training of lay magistrates is far more thorough and they are far better equipped for the job than previously.
A disadvantage of lay magistrates is that there is potential for bias as they get to know some of the prosecutors and police officers.	As less serious crimes are regularly committed locally it is often the same police officers appearing and the same CPS prosecutors. Magistrates have been shown to side too readily with these people. This can be seen by the low acquittal rate.	However, there are very few appeals against magistrates' decisions so the majority of people passing through must feel that they have been fairly treated.

2   Compare the role of juries in civil and criminal cases.

	In criminal cases	In civil cases
When used?	12 jurors in Crown Court for trials on indictment – less than 1% of criminal cases.	Used only in four types of case: defamation, false imprisonment, malicious prosecution and fraud (County and High Court). Only retained for these cases because they deal with character or reputation. Can be refused even in these cases if the judge thinks the evidence is too complicated. Allowed in personal injury cases in the High Court in exceptional circumstances. *Ward v James* but none deemed exceptional so none have had juries.
What do they do?	Listen to evidence and judge's summing up. Decide whether the defendant is guilty or not guilty.	Dual role in civil cases to decide liability and assess damages to be awarded.
What do they decide?	Only decide questions of fact not law. Do not give reasons for their decisions.	Only decide questions of fact not law. Do not give reasons for their decisions.
Unanimous?	Majority verdicts may be given – introduced to prevent jury nobbling.	Majority verdicts may be given – introduced to prevent jury nobbling.
Where does discussion take place?	Discussion takes place in secret.	Discussion takes place in secret.

Chapter 8

Now test yourself

1 Complete the following table.

Type of help	What it covers	Means or merits test?
Duty Solicitor Scheme	Available to anyone questioned at the police station but will only be by telephone unless attendance will 'materially progress the case'. Covers advice and attending interviews but attendance is limited unless the client is vulnerable.	Free to all, no means or merits testing.
Advice and assistance in criminal cases	Covers advice and preparatory work for someone charged with an offence and help with their application for legal representation limited to one hour's work. If at the Magistrates' Court – contracted solicitor with relevant qualification (Magistrates' Court Qualification) acts under the duty solicitor scheme where it is.	Means tested – only those on very low incomes qualify. Free for anyone in custody at the Magistrates' Court.
Representation in criminal cases	Covers representation and all steps in preparation of a case.	Means and merits tested.

2 Try to identify the issues in the following scenario and conclude whether the funding criteria have been applied correctly to Thomas.

- Thomas has been arrested for a serious offence and has a right to advice under the duty solicitor scheme, which is neither means nor merits tested.
- He has a limited understanding of English so a phone call, unless the duty solicitor speaks his native language, does not follow the criteria. The duty solicitor should attend in this situation as it would materially progress the case.
- At the Magistrates' Court he has correctly been given help with his bail application.

- As he is unemployed he is likely to be within the means test criteria unless he fails on the capital criteria.
- He should not be denied representation in the Crown Court; he should only have to pay contributions.
- He should pass the interests of justice test for funding as manslaughter is a serious offence with a likelihood of a custodial sentence. The fact that his English is poor is also a factor to be taken into account with this test.
- Overall the funding criteria have not been applied correctly in this case.

3 Complete the following table.

Type of help	What it covers	Means or merits test?
Civil legal help	Advice only.	Means tested.
Help at court for a civil case	Advice and help short of representation.	Means tested on disposable capital and disposable income. The limits are quite low, allowing those on income-based benefits to qualify and very few others.
Legal representation in civil cases	Legal representation at court.	Means test and merits test based on likelihood of success and amount of damages likely to be awarded and the conduct of the parties.

Exam practice answers and quick quizzes at **www.therevisionbutton.co.uk/myrevisionnotes**

G152 Answers

Chapter 1

Now test yourself

1 The case of *R v Howe* decided (ratio) that duress would not provide a defence to a charge of murder. It was also said, obiter, that duress should not provide a defence to a charge of attempted murder either. This was then followed in the later case of *R v Gotts*.

2 The Court of Appeal (Civil Division) itself, the High Court (Queen's Bench Division) and all the inferior courts.

3 Nobody – possible persuasive influence over Magistrates' Court.

4 All the UK courts will be obliged to follow the decision but they are not bound.

5 The UKSC itself and all UK courts from the UKSC down.

6 All criminal UK courts from the Court of Appeal (Criminal Division) down.

7 The UKSC has been dealing with a case on insanity. A similar case from Hong Kong was decided by the Privy Council 20 years ago. The UKSC can **choose** whether to follow the Hong Kong case as it is only **persuasive**.

8 The Court of Appeal is dealing with an unusual case concerning stealing money by hacking into a computer and transferring funds to a foreign bank account. There is no English authority on the point of law so the Court of Appeal makes an **original** precedent which future **lower** courts will now have to follow.

9 The Crown Court must follow the decision of the Court of Appeal as it is **binding**. This is because the Court of Appeal is **higher** in the hierarchy than the Crown Court.

10 Overruling

11 Distinguishing

12 Following

13 Reversing

14 Typical answers should look like this:

Point	Developed point	Well-developed point
The **Practice Statement** appears to have been met with some initial reluctance to use it. It took the House of Lords six years until they made their first serious use of their new power (**Herrington**) and statements made in **Knuller** seem to confirm this reluctance.	However, later on, increased confidence led to greater use of the Practice Statement even in areas where caution had originally been advised such as crime (**Shivpuri**) and contract (**Miliangos**).	On the other hand, many would argue that overall the Practice Statement has been rarely used since its inception and that this reflects the traditional reluctance amongst judges to be seen as law-makers and preferring Parliament to legislate where possible (**C v DPP**).

The Court of Appeal should have more power because, in reality, they are the final appeal court for most cases (note numbers and leave to appeal difficulties).	As well as this, the Court of Appeal with its 37 judges has a broader range of expertise to call on than the UKSC with 11 judges.	However, giving the Court of Appeal powers similar to the UKSC would undermine the system of precedent and create uncertainty, leaving lower courts confused about which court to follow.

Chapter 2

Now test yourself

1 Idea (G) – Initiative for new law

2 Green Paper (F) – Consultation document

3 White Paper (C) – Formal proposals

4 Bill (B) – White Paper formally drafted

5 First Reading (H) – Formal announcement

6 Second Reading (E) – Main debate

7 Committee Stage (A) – Line by line scrutiny

8 Report Stage (J) – Firm proposals

9 'Other place' (D) – Repeat process

10 Royal Assent (I) – Monarch approves

11 FALSE

12 FALSE

13 TRUE

14 TRUE

15 FALSE

16 FALSE

17 TRUE

18 FALSE

19 FALSE

20 FALSE

21 Any example from the table on page 102 will be correct but the key issue is to link the words in the statute with the reason why statutory interpretation is needed.

22 Where words are given their plain, ordinary, grammatical meaning even if it produces an absurd result.

23 In Berriman the widow could not sue for compensation despite her husband dying in an accident at work because the literal rule said what he was doing (oiling the points) was only 'maintaining' the points not 'relaying or repairing' them, which the Act requires.

24 They allow the court to avoid an absurd or repugnant outcome by varying the language used.

25 Re Sigsworth is an example of the wide golden rule because there were not two alternative meanings to choose between as happens with the narrow golden rule.

26 Mischief means fault or problem in this context and remedy means solution.

27 Heydon's Case (1584).

28 Soliciting in the street.

29 Our membership of the EU, or Common Market as it was then known.

30 Because they thought they were in the same 'genus of facts'.

Chapter 3

Now test yourself

1 One minister per Member State but a revolving membership based on the agenda.

2 Six months.

3 Their own Member State.

4 To avoid power blocs and promote co-operation.

5 The Council and the President.

6 The Parliament.

7 25,000.

8 They draft and propose new legislation.

9 754.

10 It is based on the size of the Member State's population.

11 MEPs sit in political not national groupings.

12 Parliament has an equal say to the Council in the ordinary legislative process but is only consulted in others.

13 Three – the ECJ, the General Court and the Civil Service Tribunal.

14 Advocates General.

15 Dealing with preliminary rulings.

16 A mandatory referral must be made as there is no appeal from that court's decision whereas a discretionary referral leaves the court to choose.

Check your understanding

1 Founding, amending or accession and credit any relevant examples from the table on page 116.

2 A Regulation is intended to create legislative uniformity and would, therefore, be addressed to all Member States, whereas a Directive is a harmonising measure and might only be addressed to certain Member States.

3 Direct applicability refers to whether further action needs to be taken by the Member States to enact legislation, where direct effect refers to whether a legal measure gives rise to rights which an individual can rely in the courts of his/her Member State.

4 Whether or not an organisation is an arm of the state or not.

5 The main injustice is that it gives rights to individuals in some cases but not in others even though they have the same grievance.

6 Article 4(3) TEU.

Chapter 4

Now test yourself

1 Consolidation is where a number of disparate Acts of Parliament are brought together under one Act in order to make the law in a particular area more accessible. It doesn't necessarily change the law but it makes it easier to find. An example of consolidation is the Powers of the Criminal Courts (Sentencing) Act 2000, which brought together laws on sentencing powers which were previously contained in more than a dozen Acts. Codification, on the other hand, is where all the law both common and statutory are brought together in one source. Codification would tend to be more ambitious than consolidation. An example of codification can be seen in the attempts to create a Criminal Code although Parliament has not acted on these proposals.

Check your understanding

1 Law reform is either making new laws or amending existing laws.

2 Law reform may be necessary because of government policy, obligations under EU law, Private Members' Bills; social change; moral change; changing attitudes to gender, race, age, sexual orientation, religious beliefs and disability; Public Inquiries; public opinion; pressure groups; specific interest groups; emergency situations; judicial decisions, etc.

3 The Theft (Amendment) Act 1996.

4 Homosexuality (age of consent).

5 The government through cabinet committees.

6 The Law Commission Act 1965 (as amended by the Law Commission Act 2009).

7 Five Commissioners including a Chair (usually a High Court Judge) supported by supported by a Chief Executive and about 20 members of the Government Legal Service, two Parliamentary Counsel, and a number of research assistants.

8 Repeal, Consolidation and Codification.

9 Referral, Research, Consultation and Proposal for reform.

10 Examples include the Occupier's Liability Act 1984, the Land Registration Act 2002, the Fraud Act 2006 and the Corporate Manslaughter and Corporate Homicide Act 2007.